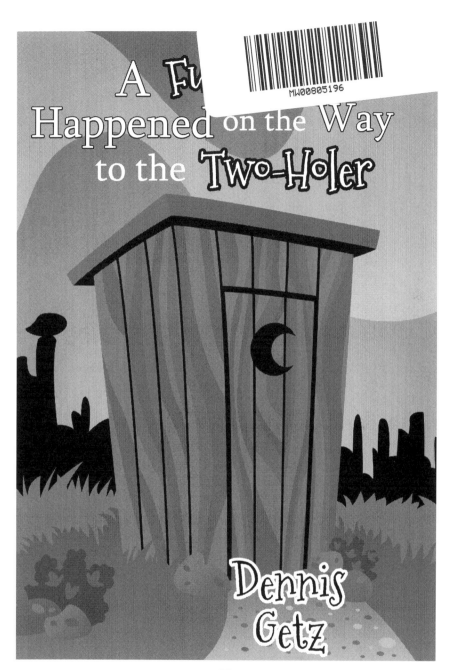

A Fu
Happened on the Way
to the Two-Holer

Dennis Getz

WINTERS
PUBLISHING

WintersPublishing.com
812-663-4948

A Funny Thing Happened on the Way to the Two-Holer

© 2013 Dennis Getz

Back cover and interior illustrations courtesy of Nathan C. Allaire

Published by:
Winters Publishing
P.O. Box 501
Greensburg, IN 47240
www.winterspublishing.com
812-663-4948

ISBN 10: 1-883651-69-7
ISBN 13: 978-1-883651-69-5

Library of Congress Control Number: 2013956574

Printed in the United States of America.

Preface

This book was written because of the author's love for literature, family, and adventure. He lived with bravado, engaged in life with vigor, and looked for the funny in everything. He was an old soul in a young man's body, who eventually became an old man with a young heart. He poured many hours into the stories you are about to read and he loved every minute: of the telling and the doing. We, his family, hope you can lose yourself in the adventures of Dennis Getz—a boy, a son, a lover, a friend, a husband, a father, a patriot, and a teller of tall tales. A Hero … these are his stories, this was his life …

Table of Contents

Introduction

Most of us, at one time or another, have encountered humorous, awkward, or unusual experiences in our lives. For whatever reason, I seem to have encountered more than my share of snafus for it to be considered normal.

I always thought it would be worthwhile to assemble an assortment of these tales, beginning with my earliest recollections, and include some that take us right up to the present. I choose to record them solely for their entertainment value and for the shell-shocked generations yet to come. The reader will discover them to be written randomly, with no intention to appear historical, as in an autobiography, which I trust will please most. If at any time anyone becomes hysterical, I gladly plead guilty to all charges.

It will be helpful to understand from the outset, and always keep in mind, that I am not up to my gunwales in modern-day "political correctness," nor do I intend to join the misery of it all. Quite frankly, the entire subject has always been an insult to my intelligence and given me a pain just south of the lumbar. It would not surprise me to learn that this form of thought control nonsense, somehow, can be traced back to Karl Marx and that crowd. Whatever, I disdain anything that wars against individuality or free self-expression.

Sadly, much of present-day society appears to have been "worked over" by this mob mentality, which stifles natural expression. Fortunately, I grew up in a time when people were not intimidated by social engineering; therefore, I have always enjoyed laughing at my circumstances and myself.

It may sound strange, but I rarely recognize the outcome of most situations, although I endeavor to "put the shoe on the other foot" each and every time, especially when it comes to the sensitive side of females.

I grew up in the small Bucks County town of Solebury, which is about four miles from the Delaware River, on the Pennsylvania side. I had an older brother, Harvey, who was nine years my senior, and a younger brother, Reggie, born seventeen months after me.

From our viewpoint, we were merely adventurous and curious country kids. As for myself, I saw my existence as an early settler taming the wilderness, subduing his adversaries, and taking few prisoners. We never purposed criminality in our happy pursuits, but I am certain a few "crimes" sprang up now and then. Ours was a "live free or die trying" way of life, and I wouldn't trade a moment of the experience with anybody in this present age.

I am certain Samuel Clemens would have recognized many of our mindless, inquisitive qualities in a heartbeat. I am also reasonably certain he would have penned volumes about our exploits, had he known about us. Come to think of it, he wrote something on the subject, which I will attempt to paraphrase, because I don't have access to the exact quote. It was something to this effect: *When a boy reaches his teens, place him in a barrel and nail the lid shut, leaving a knothole so he can breathe and you can slip him some food and water. Then, when he gets a little older, seal up the knothole!*

Most of the "education" about life, I gained from trial and error. That, to me, is what makes these stories so endearing, and I trust will capture your interest. No doubt about it, some of the mentality on display here will run smack into those who were raised on a higher plane, but there is no intention to ruffle anyone's feathers. I am a product of my upbringing, as you are yours. Perfection is tough to come by! So, let the chips fall where they may, and your imagination take over from there. Enjoy!

Lastly, I have postponed writing these articles for far too long. The Creator only gives us so much time, and I do my best storytelling conscious and upright, rather than lying on my back with my lifeless hands folded over my unpierced navel.

My Three Eels

I was meandering through my twelfth year of perpetual "mischief-making," when the fascinating idea of going fishing came to me from out of the wild blue, postponing an entire day of mediocrity. Angling was never an activity that burned in my heart of hearts, but on this particular occasion, the concept became a passion too irresistible to ignore.

Retrieving worms for bait was accomplished by overturning flagstones and putting my twitchy treasures in a baked bean can half-filled with loam. Tracking down my "fishing gear" was quite a different story. I didn't have an organized system where I kept things. It's not that I preferred scrounging; I just wasn't programmed to be a nerd.

When I finally came up with the essential gear, I boarded my robin's egg blue girl's bike, and headed four miles down a woodland dirt lane for my destination north of Center Bridge. It was not an easy journey, because I was weaving all over the road, trying to steer, while holding onto a fishing pole, a tackle box, a galvanized bucket containing my worms, and a hastily-packed lunch. Other than my "drunken" appearance to an occasional motorist, I enjoyed the downhill ride through the tall shade trees and peaceful underbrush, dotted with rhododendron and fern. Sunshine filtered through the treetops, enhancing all my aspirations for a successful outing.

I soon arrived at my journey's end, meat-hungry, and filled with anticipation. I hid my bike in the bushes, and decided to try my luck in the canal first. This waterway ran parallel to the river and was once used to tow coal barges for commerce, but hadn't been in use for close to twenty years. In mere moments I landed a small carp, which I briefly considered keeping, but released. My recollections reminded me of a time I tried to eat pan-fried carp, and the experience taught me they had a flavor somewhere between boiled sweat socks and duck muck. No amount of salted butter or lemon pepper will hide their muddy taste, and if that doesn't deter you, they have more bones than a porcupine has quills! I was never partial to them after that, and happy to give them back to Mother Nature for the crawfish and buzzards to dine on!

I quickly lost interest in the lack of action the canal served up, so I made my way through some tall brush and boulders to the river's edge. Toting all my gear and junk along about did me in, but I finished the obstacle course, found a quiet eddy off from the main channel and settled in to catch a mess of fish. After about two more hours of trying several good-looking spots and coming up empty, I began to lose my enthusiasm.

However, I regained my fishing interest when I fell upon a terrific idea, which I thought would up my odds of landing something. I concluded what I needed to do was add a few more hooks on my line. Obviously, one wiggly worm wasn't attracting enough attention, so I set about adding two more leaders and attached several large split shot sinkers. All the extra lead was enough to serve as a boat anchor, but I wanted to cast my bait farther out from the shore.

When I finally had my "rat's nest" assembled, I gave it a mighty heave out into the "briny deep." I was so proud of myself, imagining I was probably the first human being to ever concoct such an ingenious device. The cast sailed "halfway to Canada," and looked like a basketball net lashed to a tire chain. It made a thunderous splash and sank out of sight like an anvil down a sinkhole! The concussion probably sent everything with fins or claws fleeing for its life. All I had to do after the waves died down was wait for the earthworms to work their magic. ... And I waited, and I waited, and I waited, until I sensed moss was beginning to form on the north side of my body. Maybe the concussion had killed my worms. The only bites I was getting were from mosquitoes. Not one sign of aquatic life!

Eventually, I really began to lose all interest in my fishing adventure. The entire day began to take on the appearance of a total bust. I even entertained the idea of going back to the canal and fishing for carp; at least I would have had something to scale and clean, and show off to my brother. Over and above this, I was more than glad no one was depending on my fishing skills for survival. Death by starvation was a real possibility!

As my creative mind forever had a tendency to do, I came up with yet another great idea, which caused me to abandon my culinary interests, and take a walk up the hillside in search of dead trees on the other side of the road. Naturally, I placed a large rock on top of my pole; supposedly, in the rare chance something should happen to start feasting on my dead annelids, and set off on my diversion.

I always found it extremely enjoyable to hunt for dead trees to knock down. The purpose was to rock them back and forth, and see whether I could push them over. The fun of this was the noise a falling tree would make, when it smashed its way through the greenery on its way to the ground, and witnessing the destruction of everything in its path. There was the added thrill of dodging the busted off treetops when they came hurtling to the forest floor. The trick was to avoid getting your skull caved in and being agile enough to escape the falling debris. Living to tell about it was the motivation!

My brother and I spent hours doing it. We developed an ear for the cracking sounds of the brittle wood high overhead, and knew when broken pieces were overtaken by gravity. It was more of a challenge when the two of us were involved, because the two of us could take on the "monsters." There was the added adventure of not running over one another while escaping the falling debris. Once in awhile we would get pummeled, but more often than not, we would pick the right escape route.

Most of what I found on this adventure was small dead growth, but I brought down a couple of big ones as well! It never occurred to me how long it would be until someone found my lifeless body, should I draw the "short straw." Likewise, I could only imagine what the coroner or medical examiner's report would say. Probably something like this: "The deceased was found in a wooded area with a three-foot birch log protruding from his concaved skull" or "Dumb luck claims lad of 12."

After wearing myself out in the August humidity, I decided it was time to gather up my stuff and head back home. When I returned to my fishing pole, I noticed that it was no longer under the rock where it had been, but facing downstream, signaling I had probably caught something. Excitedly, I rolled the rock aside and started to reel in my prize; however, it only moved a short distance when it hit a snag. I carefully tugged on the line as hard as I dared, trying not to snap it. Surprisingly, it broke free and I reeled in again, but the line hung up once more. At this point, I began to think that all my extra "rigging" was getting snarled on the rocky bottom. I figured if I were patient, I would eventually retrieve my "rat's nest," and exuberantly skip through the May apples, like a wood nymph at a woodcutter's ball!

The situation was quite puzzling. I questioned whether I would ever find out what kind of river life I had bagged. At last, the battle neared its conclusion as I brought my catch close enough to the shoreline to see that it wasn't a branch, but a four-foot eel. When I got the swirling beast on shore, to my amazement I had another one on the second leader, and yet another on the third hook. Good grief! This was the last thing I expected or wanted.

Once the catch was landed, frustration really began to raise its ugly head. The eels twisted themselves around anything and everything they came into contact with. When I tried to get a grip on one to free it from its hook, the other two were busy encasing themselves in leaves, sticks, fishing line, and eel slime. The entire situation was a fiasco!

They were too slippery to get a good grip on to get the hooks from their gullets. Each eel had swallowed the bait to the hilt. It became apparent from the rolling, swirling mass that the predicament was beyond doing anything about. I decided to cut the line and put them in my galvanized bucket, figuring I would deal with the situation later on in life. I gathered all my stuff together, dug my bike out of hiding, and peddled for home.

If I thought I had been weaving in the road before, the uphill ride became even more of a challenge. I had to get off and push most of the way up the hill. By the time I came clattering up our driveway, the circumstances with the eels hadn't improved very much. Once inside our house, I dumped the critters in one of Mom's washtubs, filled it with water, and separated the happy trio from all the rubble. I also separated their heads from their writhing torsos on a cutting board, and skinned them with a pair of flat-nosed pliers. I was finally able to remove the fishhooks, and believe me when I tell you, I had no desire to repeat the experience ever again.

That night, I dipped the pieces in a mixture of egg and "moo juice," rolled them in cornmeal, and fried them to a golden brown. They turned out to be very tasty, although I'm not sure they were worth all the trouble I went to.

The story I just told you is only the opening salvo in a long list of frustrating fishing adventures that soured my affection for the sport. Oh sure, I've had an occasional good time, now and then, but when I weigh that against all the lures I've lost, the overturned tackle boxes, sunburns, mosquito maulings, lost fishing equipment, wasted gasoline, lunches left at home, bait cans dumped overboard, poison ivy, leeches, tree snags, snarled fishing lines, reel backlashes, catching nothing all day and watching everybody else fill their creels, capsized boats and canoes, lost oars, going over dams and waterfalls with or without a boat beneath me, wading through mud up past your knees, waders filling up with water, cascading down slippery embankments, plunging headlong into raging currents, canoes pinned against log jams, expensive fishing licenses, expensive expired fishing licenses, being chased by dogs, being chased by bulls, being chased by angry property owners, arguments over who got there first, docks collapsing, getting drenched in surprise storms, digging fish hooks out of my hide, sea sickness, knife wounds, stink bait, getting gored by catfish, getting lost, and explaining where you were and what took you so long. These things have distanced me from the love I once thought I had for the pastime.

I get all my fish at the market these days, and sometimes at Lenten fish fries. It makes more sense that way.

Celery Salt

My wife, Mary Lou, and I were speeding westward on I-80, bound for the tulip festival in Pella, Iowa. Our two young offspring, Gretchen and Otto, were busy entertaining themselves in the back of our "rust-bucket" '72 Rambler station wagon, playing their favorite guessing games, as we were all anticipating the excitement of a holiday picnic and tulip show.

It was a lovely spring morning and everyone's spirits were high. We had been on the road a good hour when I turned to my wife and asked what she had in the picnic basket to munch on. Like a cat, she whirled around on the front seat and began to rummage around in the back seat where the "booty" was stashed, and after a few moments turned to me and dutifully announced, "I have cheese crackers, peanut butter cookies, apples, celery, carrot sticks, and hard-boiled eggs."

I processed the menu through my brain and settled on celery. "I'll have celery," I replied. With that, she whirled around once more and engaged in a more intense form of rummaging. In time, she came up with two long stalks of celery and a salt shaker, and proceeded to hand them to me, while I was clutching the steering wheel, busily focused upon staying in my lane, and more importantly, on the road! I say *clutching*, because the old heap had two front tires so out of alignment and balance, navigating any highway over 50 mph was like driving down the center of the Rock Island Line!

"Lou!" I frantically stated. "I'm almost going 70. I can't salt celery and keep this "Junker" on the road at the same time!" Evidently, the exasperation in my voice indicated to Mary Lou that her ambition to please had fallen on hard times, because, without uttering a word, I could sense she was seeking a solution. I watched her out of the corner of one eye, while staring at the dotted lines whizzing by, taking note that she had rolled down the front window and thrust a celery stick outside with one hand, salting it with the saltshaker.

Now, folks! I may not have all my ducks in a row or catch on to every nuance that the world throws my way, but I have gleaned a few tidbits from the halls of physics class from my days upon this planet, and the activity taking place on my right was a shade too much, for even this dumb German to endure. I *whirled* around this time, and asked, "What on earth are you doing?"

In the calmest, matter-of-fact and most sincere voice Mary Lou could manage, she answered me, "I don't want to get salt in the car!"

"I guess you don't want to get any on the celery either?" I shot back. Right away, I could tell I hadn't scored any points on the "charm meter" with that exchange.

I pulled over to the side of the road, secured the shaker and celery, took matters into my own hands, and proceeded on down the highway.

I knew instinctively that an icy silence had replaced the jovial merriment we had enjoyed only a few minutes previously. I mulled over the cardinal sin of any relationship—that of demonstrating frustration or acting short. I began to feel badly for my outburst and searched for the right words in offering an apology, because I understood that she had meant well.

I kept replaying the scene that I had just witnessed over and over in my mind. The more I thought about it, the funnier it became, until I began to snicker to myself, and finally I let out a big laugh which included a "Pusctch!" and a spray of spit. This, in turn, caused my wife to ask what was so funny.

I don't know what I said, but it broke the ice, and we both began to laugh and snicker together. This made the apology much easier and we were soon "back on track." We went on to have a very enjoyable outing. The tulips were everything we expected, and we even found a great picnic table in the park. The kids wore themselves out on the play equipment until it was time to head on home.

To this day, I still catch myself chuckling over that celery incident. Imagine going 70 mph and trying to salt anything outside the car window! It's a classic!

Hey! I wonder if it works at night?

Bike Ramp

You have to wonder how some kids ever live long enough to become teenagers, let alone adults. It can baffle parents for life, considering some of the hair-brained stunts they come up with. Take, for instance, the time I was about ten. Some of the Wilson kids, my brother, and I decided to make a ramp to see how far and high we could vault our bicycles. Now, I realize you may not be impressed, here, with the concepts of originality at present, but I am talking about a day and time long before mountain bikes, pipelines, knee pads, and helmets were ever heard of.

It all began innocently enough, when Henry Wilson (the little creep) barreled over a small hill at the Solebury Elementary School, and both wheels of his bike came off the ground. Quick to embellish his "super-human" accomplishment, word spread, as Henry made much more out of his feat than the situation warranted. Before long, all the neighborhood kids were trying to duplicate Henry's attempt at "moon launches" on all the embankments around the school. Try as we may, nobody could equal or excel the description of his miraculous endeavor; thus, since he was the youngest and dumbest in the pecking order, his biased boasting needed to be silenced.

Therefore, the wheels of adolescent invention kicked into gear. We began to scratch our heads to come up with an idea to propel our rickety bikes high off the ground. Our search of the school grounds produced a pile of cinder blocks and two twelve-foot wooden planks. We placed two cinder blocks, side by side, at the crest of a small incline, and rested the planks on the top of each block. Then one brave soul ripped across the parking lot, roared up the planks and flew past the blocks; his was NOT going to be a Kitty Hawk experience when the blocks collapsed from the impact of my front wheel. The sponge-like plank caved downward and pitched to one side. It was like riding a log flume, because when the cinder blocks disassembled, the second plank kicked up under the bike frame, catapulting me like I was on a see-saw.

I became airborne in grand style, all right, but nothing like the magnificent falcon I had recently envisioned. I'm thinking I looked more like a dead mallard, laced with thirty pounds of buckshot. There was nothing graceful about it by any stretch of anybody's imagination! I slammed to earth, still clutching the handlebars for dear life, but my sorry carcass was three feet above the bicycle seat. When I rejoined the bike, I landed on the crossbar square! From then on everything became a black and blue blur, with a few shades of green, and an occasional glimpse of blue sky. I cascaded head over heels so many times I must have resembled a disconnected windmill, and in conclusion, bounced and rolled like a Hudson hubcap on the freeway.

I came to rest several yards from where it all began and I couldn't speak for what seemed an eternity. I'm certain I resembled a stranded catfish gasping for any breath I could get, but that was a good sign!

A sudden mood swing came over the happy gathering. There were no more "takers" at the four-block level from then on. In fact, as I remember it, bike ramps were never seen again, in those parts, for the rest of my days.

Outside of the fact that the only damage to my bike was a bent front fender, I considered myself fortunate. It took awhile for the agony to subside and my breathing to regain normalcy, and no bones were broken.

That's also how I became a tenor to my dying day!

Taking the Offering

This story will be difficult to compose because parts of it came to me from second-hand informants. The remainder will be supplied by vague recollections of my brother and me, who were four to six years of age at the time of this account.

It is important to understand that, early on in life, my brother and I were devout hedonists. Not by design, mind you, but due to the absence of sound guidance and direction, which was interspersed with a generous outpouring of spankings inflicted upon us by our dad, who was the chief corrections officer, attempting to head off our self-destruction.

Because we survived the first 100 and were still alive, the 101st descended on us like crows on a flat cat in the middle of the road, a natural progression in our barbaric march to reach age seven. Adding to this the realization that we were only a heartbeat away from destitution, our yearning hearts were open to any sign of affection from the human race.

Who should burst upon this endemic scene, but none other than our dear Aunt Elsie, who found it in her heart to expose us to some "church learnin'." I believe it was her perception that if we didn't run into some divine intervention anytime soon, we would be swinging hammers and doing hard time among real heathens!

Thus, dressed in our finest rags, she saw to it that we were swooped up and deposited at the local Trinity Episcopalian Church, right there in downtown Solebury, and not a minute too soon; because ol' Satan was just itching to get us side-tracked into another round of hooliganism.

To be honest, we didn't have the foggiest notion of church life in those days, and apparently, neither did Aunt Elsie, because she didn't waste any time, and spoke in lingo foreign to my ears; which everybody seemed to agree with, because they all answered back in English a few times. While all this was going on, another dude was swinging a smoking cannonball around, like he was after something, spouting the same sort of gibberish. None of this made any sense either!

Next thing I knew, this huge gold plate full of money came a-dancing by. Apparently, they were giving moola away. Instinctively, I grabbed a handful and passed it on to my brother, who had the most astonished, bug-eyed gaze you'll ever see on a four-year-old! He picked out a big shiny fifty-cent piece and handed the plate to the lady next to him. We were grinning from ear to ear. No wonder the place was so packed out. No wonder everybody was so anxious to get down on the floor and grovel, there really was money down there! That explained a lot!

The lady sitting beside my brother was sporting a large white chicken hat. I knew that because of the feathers sticking out of it in every direction. She was giving us the most stoic stare, the likes of which would have killed a weasel at fifty yards. I guessed she was mad because she probably had her eyes on the fifty-cent piece Ronnie had clutched in his grimy mitts! She snatched the plate away from him and passed it on down the pew. I noticed she didn't take anything, so I figured she was just a sore loser.

Wow! What a friendly place! Wild Indians and poison snakes couldn't have kept us away from there after an experience like that! Up until then, I never had more than a couple of pennies to my name, and most of that I found lying in the street. I always wondered where people got their loot, which explained why Pop never had any! He avoided church like a tomcat fleeing gunfire!

Well, I tell you what! The very next Sunday, we didn't need Aunt Elsie to come take us to our happy hunting ground. We were up at the crack of dawn, dressed in our favorite rags, and walked the three-quarters of a mile to church on our own. My mind reeled, thinking about all the Hershey bars you could buy at five cents a pop!

Sure as you were born, our devotion paid off. They had the same parade and rigamarole all over again, and they were handing out the money just like marshmallows at a Girl Scout campout. If we would have gotten wind of this program sooner, we would have gone through them church doors as soon as we were weaned, with or without Aunt Elsie's concern.

However, a strange thing happened on this second visit to the hallowed "halls of cabbage." We were sitting on the end of our row, waiting for the offering with great expectations, but when it was our turn, the plates were passed over our heads and on to the row behind us. We looked at each other and didn't say anything, but I wanted to tell somebody that we weren't intending to be wasteful!

Meaning, we only wanted to snag enough to keep us in candy and bubble gum for nine months. I am proud to announce that we weren't greedy in the least. We would happily spend every cent they gave us and help out the free enterprise system with the merriest of hearts!

Stranger yet was when we went back a few weeks later. A stern-looking man, dressed in a black suit, met us at the entranceway when we came tearing up the front steps. We were like two racehorses rarin' to go by this time! He looked at us harshly and said that we weren't welcome, grabbed us by our arms, and marched us to the end of the driveway. We were crestfallen because we had lost our "cash cow" and weren't sure why.

The man seemed so unhappy with us that we left, dutifully, and never went back to church again. What was so odd was no one ever mentioned to us what we did that was wrong. We figured it out with the passing of time, but we were glad that Pop never found out about it or we would have gotten spanking #102.

At the time, I tried to tell my brother that it was all his fault. He should have left that half-dollar alone and stuck to the green stuff like I did, but that was just so much nonsense, was it not?

Grape Soda, Anyone?

Just before I graduated from sixth grade and the torment of "Old Mommy" Mason, I became a member of the Solebury Elementary Safety Patrol. The only reason I get all choked up over the experience is, prior to that time in my life, I was never chosen for anything with even this much responsibility.

Looking back, I haven't the slightest idea how I could have risen to such heights of honor. I know I didn't volunteer. I cannot imagine anyone recommending me, nor do I recall accomplishing anything to validate my membership. The only possibility remaining was some do-gooder invented a statute and forced me to join, beyond my ability to protest.

I was only on Patrol a few months, at best, and my duties were to assist the regular crossing guard before and after school. I can still recall the vital role I played in the operation. "Stay out of the way and try not to get run over!" I was told.

I wore a white belt that went around my waist, with a diagonal strap that went over my right shoulder and fastened in the back. It had bold black letters emblazoned on it, which read "SAFETY PATROL."

When this torturous tenure of citizenship ran its course, I was awarded a certificate and a ticket to attend a baseball game at Schibe Park, between the then despised Brooklyn Dodgers, and our beloved Philadelphia Phillies. Receiving the news that I would actually be at a major league baseball game to boo the Dodgers, and cheer on the "Whiz Kids," was a dream of the highest calling. Nobody in our family rooted for the "Bums," but we had our share of traitors who made the trip!

The event was in conjunction with all the other Safety Patrols in the Philadelphia area and was an annual affair. I had never been to a Phillies game before, and the expectations were more than a country boy could handle. Game day seemed to take forever to arrive, but in June of 1953, I found myself seated with all my classmates, in the upper deck out in right field, waiting for the start of the donnybrook.

We had arrived in time for batting practice, but like all kids at that age, we were sidetracked with everything but the goings on down on the field. The excitement of the moment had us all whipped into a lather, and it was probably the first time I had ever been on my own at a social function. To top it off, I was with my best friend in the entire world, Terry. I don't know what it is with certain personalities, but when you mix them together, the human race usually suffers a setback. Whenever we got together, I would undergo a transformation from being a general irritation into a hardcore nuisance. He infected my common sense and altered my reasoning powers, ever since I first knew him. I became another person; acting silly and doing things I would never think of performing on my own. This occasion would be no exception and I was helpless to alter my condition.

You would think I would have been focused on the game, because somewhere in that happy throng down below were Gil Hodges, "Jackie" Robinson, Robin Roberts, Willie "Puddin' Head" Jones, and my hero, Richie Ashburn. But, no! I was too occupied with entertaining myself and everybody else around.

Somewhere along the line, I had been given some spending money, and had just returned from the refreshment stand with a gigantic cup of grape soft drink. It was much more than I could possibly drink at one sitting; however, I quieted myself and began to sip on the fruity beverage. By now, the ballgame was moving right along; most of the kids had settled down and most were interested in the contest, but it may have well been a mud fight for all the attention Terry and I were giving it.

From out of nowhere, he suggested, "I dare you to dump your soda over the railing." We kidded back and forth about it a few times, because actually "doing that" was the last thought on my mind. But, guess what I did?

Over the railing went the purple rain! We watched it as gravity came into play, and it collided with several empty seats below, splattering in every direction of the compass. Indiscriminately, the sugary soda "sought out" several unsuspecting spectators, causing them to scatter for cover, particularly a stout middle-aged man with a Dodger pennant.

Hilarity broke out in the upper regions of the stands where Terry and I were seated, as curious classmates and bystanders were fascinated about the outcome of the fulmination down below. Merrily, we all peered down into the irritated faces scurrying around. Of particular interest was one pair of dagger-glazed eyes belonging to the said middle-aged man, wearing a blue baseball cap with the familiar "B" displayed on it, who was engaged in frantically wiping himself off with a hanky. He kept looking our way, displaying a clenched fist, and spouting a string of strongly-worded personal indignities.

This crude behavior alerted my delicate nature to the fact that death by strangulation and disfiguration was rampant in this man's New York City heart. The reality of the situation was magnified when the red-faced man shouted, "One of you rotten kids is gonna' pay for that!" With this endearing salutation, we all sat back down and ceased peering over the railing.

In human nature, when one knows that one has gone over the line, it is most interesting to observe that the first thing one tries to do is justify the wrongdoing. I knew instinctively that the enraged man was probably making his way up to our section, with the distinct intention of "killing" one of us, so I turned to Terry and told him, "If he comes up here, I'll just say it was an accident."

Terry shot back, "When he gets here you won't have time to explain anything!"

"How's he going to know who did it?" I asked.

My best friend in the entire world said, "Because I'll tell him it was you. I ain't getting my brains beat out! I want to see the rest of the game. If I were you, I'd get out of here while you still can."

Realizing he probably would betray me in less time than it would take to swat a horsefly, I began to picture how brief my short life might be and how brutally it could end. Would it be by strangulation, as two sticky hands crushed my esophagus? Or would

I be bludgeoned to death by a hot dog vendor's tongs? Maybe I would be dragged to the concession stand and drowned in a vat of grape soda? Perhaps it would end by a crazed madman hurling me over the upper deck railing, and an irate mob of Dodger lovers stomping me into eternity? None of these options appealed to me!

Just then, I heard a distant voice calling my name. It was my best friend in all the world reminding me that he was sure the "madman" would be here any time. "You better get out of here," he said again.

With that, I started up the steps for the exit. About halfway to the first landing, I passed a stern-looking guy who seemed to be on a mission. Right after we raced past each other, I heard his angry voice shout, "Which one of you scum balls doused me with soda?"

Almost in unison, the entire Solebury Elementary Safety Patrol turned and pointed their traitorous fingers in my direction and eagerly volunteered, "There he goes!!!"

The jig was up! "Come back here, you lousy punk!" came the voice from the rear. I immediately sent my legs into overdrive and set out for parts unknown. I made the second landing and kept on going, knowing full well my pursuer was in hot pursuit, as I heard several more versions of his death threats close behind. I tried to lose him among the maze of iron girders and vacant seats. I even climbed halfway up a monstrous iron gate, when a security guard ordered me to stop and to get down right away.

When I descended, he asked what I was trying to do, commit suicide? I told him that some kids were after me and I was trying to get away. The guard insisted that I go back to my seat and added, "If there is any more trouble, I will take care of it."

Well, I knew better than to head directly back into the teeth of the storm, so I milled around the upper reaches of the stadium for quite awhile. There was nothing but empty seats, and I had a good vantage point to keep a sharp eye out for the crazed maniac, but I soon grew anxious to rejoin my cohorts of mayhem. Nervously, I made my way back to our section and slinked down the many steps where the giddy throng awaited.

When I finally sat down, Terry was laughing up a storm at my predicament, but I was in no mood for merrymaking at that juncture.

He said to me, "It's a good thing you vamoosed when you did. That guy showed up right after you left. He would have skinned you alive!"

"Yeah, I know. I passed him on the steps. He could have grabbed me, but he must not have recognized me," I said.

"Yeah, ha-ha-ha! We turned around and saw him running after you! Ha-ha-ha! Did he catch you?"

I recounted the tale from that point and included an embellished description of my gate-climbing experience with the security guard, just to give my famous exploits some flair.

To this day, I don't remember whether the Phillies won or lost that day. More than likely they took one on the chin. I don't even recall how we got home or much of anything else. All of that has been lost with the passing of time. I suppose one can salvage a bit of humor from the telling of this story, but to my credit, I never tried a stunt like that again. However, that wasn't the last time a friend got me into trouble. Someone once told me that it would be best to pal around with our enemies and detractors. They may cause you trouble, but nine times out of ten, they won't coax you into it!

Parakeet History

Less than a year after I moved away from home and the serene, bird-chirping countryside of rural Bucks County, I rented an upstairs apartment on Cherry Street in Willow Grove. The new living quarters, at first, were "unfurnished to the hilt," which was very much to my liking.

I was experiencing life from the bottom up. After my first 23 years, I had managed to crawl out from underneath the rock I had been under, and I didn't care to be interrupted on the rest of my upward ascent. Unlike a lot of young folks who were starting out, I did not "inherit the Earth" from Mom and Dad. I knew a few of these spoiled counterparts and I had difficulty relating to them. In their way of thinking, if a place wasn't on ground level, didn't feature wall-to-wall carpeting, a two-car garage, and air-conditioning—"It wasn't fit to live in!"

Me? I was as ecstatic as a mouse in a corncrib, just to have a place with a light switch and one outlet to a room, windows with panes, glass doorknobs, and gutters for the rain to run into; that was good enough for me! I was reared without frills. If I had to navigate a dark hallway, climb a flight of creaky stairs, or park my car two-and-a-half blocks away? So what! If the floors were as bald as a bowling alley, the doors stuck to the jams, flypaper dangled from the ceiling, and the humidity was high enough to grow moss on the curtains and windowsills? That's life! I liked simplicity and green things anyway!

I relished the clicking sound of my heels on the hardwood floors. It made me think I was well to do and lived in a mansion or a mausoleum. I reasoned the echoes would awaken me if someone wanted to mug me in the middle of the night! I even thought the racket made the roaches nervous, if I had any. I loved the idea of opening the windows to let "fresh air" in, or allowing the smoke to escape during the grease fires. The flies and blood-sucking bats I could kill! The open windows offered an additional feature of inviting in a chorus of barking dogs, crying babies, loud-mouthed kids, roaring motorcycles, neighborhood arguments, and cat fights. It all reminded me of how much I missed the chirping birds of the hinterland. Along with the commuter train that rumbled past every twenty minutes, the entire ruckus became an aphrodisiac, of a sort, after the lights were out!

The family who occupied the downstairs consisted of a middle-aged woman, who would have blended nicely as one of Charles Dickens's street characters. She was very small, hunched over, and very bow-legged. Her black and silver hair was always wild and unkempt. She usually appeared as if she had just survived a tornado, had been mauled by rabid dogs, or spent the night on spin cycle in a clothes dryer. Oh, yes! She had a wardrobe to match every experience!

As I said, she was one of those Dickens-like characters you would find begging outside a tavern, or selling Scrooge's bedclothes to a skinflint in hovel town. She had a chunky daughter about 15 and twin sons about 12. We got along handsomely as our personalities blended well. The only bothersome exception was that the mother always wanted to know what I was up to. She was forever asking me what I did the night before, where I was going, or when was I returning to my abode.

I thought her inquisitiveness was due to her maternal interests, more than being a busybody, but perhaps I suffered from an acute overdose of stupidity and a bad case of youthful naivete. I didn't resent her concerns; after all, I was a young bachelor with a full head of steam. I did have a few girlfriends milling around in those days. Maybe she was worried one of them would hogtie me, drag me down the aisle, and she would lose her prize renter.

Everything I owned came from Goodwill Industries. All of it probably should have been piled into a dumpster and hauled to a landfill or a ceremonial bonfire! There was a red Formica kitchen table that had been hacked up from years of cleaning fish, or two toreadors had used it as a "cape" in a bullfight. The frame was bent, causing the tabletop to slope to the center. Anything spilled on it would race to the middle crack and drip onto the floor.

I had one of the ugliest green lounge chairs you will ever lay eyes on. One side looked like it had been chewed up by bulldogs or had taken a few rounds from a ten-gauge, but I always kept that side to the wall. After all, I had some dignity in my warped sense of values.

I had a rickety dresser that I brought from home. It was the only thing I had that was actually mine. Although it had been made with Chinese slave labor, three of the four drawers worked rather well. There was a large shipping crate that served as a coffee table. I put an oval doily on it to give it a homey touch.

The last item worth mentioning was a black and white Admiral television set that had three channels and a set of huge rabbit ears, which sometimes served as an indoor clothesline. That TV had more lines running through it than a farmhouse screen door; and it had probably been slammed a few more times than the door!

For companionship, I laid out good money for a blue and yellow parakeet. I kept him in a scruffy-looking birdcage in the living room, also a Goodwill treasure. I named him PT, because I wasn't certain how to spell Petey. Was it Petie, Peety, or Peaty? For some oddball reason I didn't care for Pete, so I didn't give him that name. Go figure, if you have a lot of time to kill!

We were happy together, the two of us. I taught him to walk up my fingers, sit on my shoulder, and pick birdseed out of my earlobe. Hey! There was time for that sort of thing! Every afternoon when I came home from my job at Honeywell, I would let PT out of his cage and he would fly around the apartment like a Corsair after a Zero. It got so he would hear me creaking up the "mausoleum stairs" and break into a twittering dither. Any stranger might think I had an aviary upstairs if they had heard the noise. He probably recognized my foot pattern on the steps.

One warm spring day, when I came home from one of my jaunts, I noticed the window at the top of the stairs was open. Breezes were blowing the curtains like sails on a schooner. I guessed that the "rag-picker" wanted a cross breeze, because her front rooms faced the sunny side of the street. Without another thought, I put my burdens down and went to PT's cage to let him out. As expected, the parakeet flew around the living room a few times and made a swoop or two toward the kitchen. At that point, I remembered the kitchen door was wide open and so was the window in the hall. THE WINDOW IN THE HALL!!! If PT discovered that, he would be parakeet history!

To head him off, I raced into the kitchen, grabbed the kitchen door, and gave it a mighty slam. What dreadful timing! Just as the door slammed shut, sealing off his departure, the little bird arrived at the door jam. In the twinkling of an eye, PT was transformed from a happy, fluttering parakeet into a one-eighth-inch-thick spray of feathers! In my heart of hearts I hoped that PT had made it past the door, but a protruding wing betrayed all my degraded hope. When I opened the door, a cascade of colorful feathers fell to the floor, like so many blue and yellow snowflakes. I was stunned at the suddenness of it all. It was as if his little lifeless wing had waved one last goodbye. The best scenario for PT, relatively speaking, might have been to dry him out and make a shoehorn from his remains, as a tribute to the last trick he ever performed!

I suppose you may not find this ending all that funny, and I guess I'm not laughing either. I think because I struggled so much with his name, his demise was entirely my fault. Petey, Peaty, Peedy, or PT, what did any of that really matter? I should have just called him Slim or better yet, Slim Slam!

Kennedy Restroom and the Mystery Woman

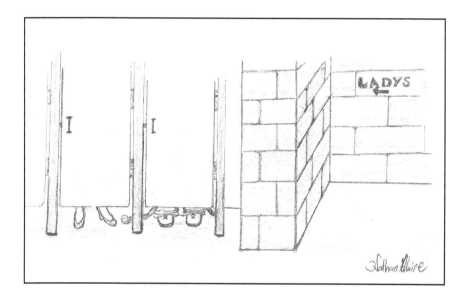

My wife, Mary Lou, and I were in attendance at Kennedy High School in the spring of 1987 for either a concert or a play. It was nearing intermission, when dread of all dreads; I had to use the restroom.

The thought of inconveniencing myself in the middle of the shindig was irritating enough, but choosing to endure a mad dash for the men's room at "halftime," amid a bison-like stampede was not, and never has been, my ideal concept of answering nature's call! I would have much preferred the serene solitude of a cornfield or straddling a fallen tree somewhere between Keokuk and Oshkosh in the dead of winter, than frequent a public facility and endure the smell and sounds of a "communal barnyard"; but I applied the customary "Excuse Me's" and sashayed past a sea of bony knees, making my way for my destination all the same.

It seems ironic, having been raised a quasi-barbarian, and also serving in the Air Force, that I would suffer such an aversion for the subject at hand, but evidently there is a sensitive side to my nature. At any rate, there I was, slithering out of the auditorium and down the hallways in search of a signpost signaling the end of my impassionate journey. Good fortune smiled on me as I came upon a restroom sign protruding from a corridor wall.

Quick as a bunny, I instinctively ducked into the first door I came to, occupied a random stall, and commenced shedding my drawers. "Oh, precious solitude. How glorious is thy habitation!" became my all-encompassing thought.

I no more than settled into my situation, when I heard the outside door open and someone entering my hallowed sanctuary. That someone, not only came into the "outhouse," but also sat down in the stall right next to me. "For crying out loud," I murmured and complained, "the purpose of this operation was to buy a few moments of solitude in this madcap world. What rotten luck! Why couldn't that fool at least pick another jug? Why did he have to sit right next to me, for Pete's sake? There are plenty of other stools!" Knowing life isn't always fair and things don't usually go the way we hope they will, I resolved to finish my project and get back to the auditorium. It was at that point I glanced down at the floor and noticed that the "fool" in the adjoining stall was wearing a dainty black-sequined, high-heeled pump, which prompted my very next thought to be, "Good night in the morning! Some idiot woman is in the wrong restroom! Can't she read signs?"

At the same moment in time, I noticed that my black belt was boldly lying across the white-tiled floor into the stall that this "fool" had occupied, and do you know what? It is amazing how quickly some guys can assemble a series of thoughts, process the information, and arrive at a conclusion, without much time going off the clock! In certain situations, it would rival lightning striking a manure pile, while the bedazzled farmhand is still holding the smoldering shovel the pile is connected to.

At the moment, I was so wishing I really was straddling a hollow log in the middle of nowhere, rather than the pristine porcelain jug

I was perched upon. Albeit, the very next blinding brain flash gave birth to the realization that the "fool" next to me probably hadn't lost her vision either, and was making similar evaluations about my belt as I had; only her pulse rate, most likely, was exceeding that of Feetlebaum, barreling down the homestretch at Garden State Parkway, with a 400-pound jockey on board.

My gray matter began to picture an ugly perception of the immediate future. I pictured spending the rest of the night in the Linn County Jail, with Gazette headlines reading "Police Nab Pervert," subtitled "Screaming Woman Fingers Restroom Deviant."

I instinctively knew, right or wrong, there was no time for a hearing or further deliberation, and I had better "shake and bake" my carcass from the premises; although there was still an outside chance the character in the next stall might be clinging to the idea that I just happened to be a "crazy broad" with odd taste in apparel … Nah!!

Stealthily, I reached down and retrieved my errant clothing, rose up and assembled myself as quickly as my nervous fingers could do it. I opened the stall door a smidge and peeked out. Deeming it safe, I vaulted for the exit like a weasel dodging a foxhound, all the while praying no one would notice my escape.

Thanks be to God, I got out of there with all my honor intact, and to this day, I can only fantasize what went on in the mind of that innocent creature sitting there, contemplating who knows what; wondering whether she would see the next dawn that dark and fateful night!

So, let me offer a brief word of advice, fellows! There are two types of "animals" out there—pointers and setters. If you are in a strange setting, make sure you follow the right crowd. Pay attention to details!

Cuttalossa Dam

Whenever I revisit my reveries, certain tales seem very vivid and the episodes quite clear, while others require my mind to search tirelessly for details and the time incidents took place. Sometimes, reflections of the days gone by can be a bit hazy, but not this one. My younger brother and I would have been 11 and 12, and it was the summer of 1954.

Solebury, at that time, was still a very quiet rural town. There were no community swimming pools, as most of you would be acquainted with in this day and age, but even if there was a pool, my brother and I wouldn't have had the money or the means to avail ourselves of one.

It was common for the summers in Eastern Pennsylvania to wax hot and sultry. I am positive that this fit of nature prompted us to build a swimming hole on nearby Cuttalossa Creek, the site of which just happened to be a few hundred yards from where our grandfather, Amos Armitage, had once operated a gristmill until 1936.

When our "construction" began, we started hatching all sort of plans. This "baby" was going to rival the Grand Coulee. We were going to stock it with fish so we could go fishing anytime we wanted, with no forethought of how many hours it would take to accomplish the feat. There was going to be a high-diving board, where we most likely would have split our skulls open on the rocks below, probably to the delight of all the townsfolk, if that had ever become a reality! We intended to build a raft and take people for rides, and fantasized charging all the neighborhood kids to go swimming, which would have been a trick Houdini would have marveled at. In addition, we were going to set up a zoo with all the animals we were going to capture and put in cages, as an attraction for rubberneckers. All this, and more was the incentive to motivate us in our building project. Why, there wasn't a Brink's truck big enough to hold all the money we were going to make!

We piled up rocks for hours, transforming the quaint, rippling, meandering stream into a huge pond on one side and a roaring tumult exiting the other. Where breaches occurred, we stuffed the ruptures with brush, muck, and small stones. Eventually, we built a fairly good-sized dam that became more than waist-deep, but there were several problems developing. For one, we had to venture farther upstream for our rocks. Big flat stones worked best, but they were challenging to transport as the water level rose. Another situation, which began to frustrate us, was the force of the backed-up water; it kept washing out sections of our dam. We began to spend more time repairing what we had already done than adding to the depth. We solved this by adding stones to the base of the dam on the exposed side, but we soon grew weary of our efforts and decided to return the next day. With renewed vigor and a stiff upper lip, we reasoned we would come back and finish our masterpiece and become the envy of all kid-building projects anywhere.

However, misfortune reared its ugly head; a thunderstorm came up that night, and when the rain torrent hit our diversion, it forced the runoff out over the creek banks, down across the adjacent meadow, gouging out a path of destruction as it escaped captivity. Unfortunately, there was a humble dwelling of a longtime property owner nestled at the base of the sleepy hillside, a short distance downstream from our "construction site." Unbeknownst to the sleeping inhabitants of the sleepy little woodland property, bedlam was breaking loose around their sleepy little beds, as the patter of rain in the sleepy little night wore on. Amid the crash of thunder and the flashes of lightning, rolling boulders and tumbling logs zeroed in on their graceful, well-manicured lawn, which was fast becoming a mobile, undulating junkyard. This raging cascade chiseled a canyon through their front yard and filled this guy's Victorian-style garage and lovely, white-tiled swimming pool with tons of rock, mud, logs, lawn chairs, gravel, brush, park benches, and a wide assortment of clawing, crushed, dying, and fleeing wild life! Not to mention their basement, porch, greenhouse, Austin-Healey, and two other cars incurred a similar decorating scheme, of which I'm certain, sent waves of joy and adoration up their spines when dawn dawned!

When we came back in a week or so, we discovered that our "swimming hole" was completely gone, and only a trace of our project was noticeable. In fact, the entire dam area looked much the same, as it would have when the Delaware Indians lived there. The rippling stream was gurgling along pretty much the way it had been the moment we first hatched the bright idea of building our mud hole, and we never gave rebuilding another thought; and besides, by the manner in which the embankment had been torn out, we needed to find another location!

It wasn't until several years after I had been out of high school, I chanced to overhear a conversation between two elderly gentlemen one day. I was sitting on the steps outside of the Post Office, reading a letter I had received. As I sat there, the two were sharing a tragic story about a "surprise flash flood" down on the Cuttalossa. From the gist of their conversation, the mention of 1954, and the freak nature of the creek-changing course, my memory flashed back in time and I started to put the pieces of their tale together.

For the first time, I realized our childhood "engineering marvel" had given anybody any grief. However, as I wasn't really certain my conclusions carried any weight, I decided not to stick around and ask questions, because they seemed to be too expensive to inquire about.

'51 Fords Can Fly

Unforgettable! Miraculous! Brainless!

These are only a few words that come to mind when I reflect on what I am about to tell you. The fact that no one was killed or seriously injured on the day in question can only be attributed to God in Heaven, who willed it otherwise.

I suspect many adults can recall something that they were implicated with, in their youth, which should have ended in disgrace and tragedy, due to poor judgment or a thoughtless act on their part. In this case, although I can look back and see the humor in it, I fully understand the seriousness of what could have occurred.

It was a dreary, drizzly day late in the autumn of 1961. I was in my nineteenth year and out "tooling around" with a long-time friend and classmate of mine. I was driving a blue 1951 Ford convertible, the first car I ever owned. I hadn't had my driver's license any more than a month or two. Both of us had just finished filing for unemployment at the county Job Service and had the rest of the day to ourselves. Our objective was to see the sights and travel back to northern New Jersey, some 50 to 60 miles north of where we were, and get Teddy back home. I was navigating in that general direction, taking roads I was unfamiliar with, intending to end up where landmarks would set our bearings straight.

As was usually the case when we got together, we were talking and laughing incessantly, and enjoying one another's company. I was traveling on a two-lane blacktop when I came to the crest of a very long hill, and as the young have a tendency to do, I wanted to impress Ted with how skillful a driver I was becoming. So, I accelerated on the downgrade to inject a bit of excitement into our lives, thus demonstrating a bit of the daredevil in myself. For the sake of this conversation, I would say that I was going a smidgeon over the posted speed limit. This condition changed my focus of attention and forced me to concentrate on keeping my junk heap in the middle of the road. When we reached the bottom of the hill I noticed we were coming to a bridge, which didn't cause me any concern, but what I failed to recognize was the bridge happened to be a camelback. The next thing I knew, we were sailing through the air like Joie Chitwood!

If you would, allow me to interrupt your thoughts for a moment and let's leave things up in the air, so to speak, for I wish to interject a little historical info.

(The camelback bridge got its name from the style from which they were constructed. In colonial times, these single-arched spans were built over small streams with a rainbow appearance to them and keystones in the center to give them strength. These bridges were fine in the days of wagons and carts, because most travelers were not in any big hurry! Courtesy was usually shown because most bridges were only wide enough for one wagon anyway.

Camelbacks were throwbacks to a style of bridge built in England long before the settlers came to America. They became fairly common in the colonies, because granite fieldstone was abundant and widely used in the construction. However, when the automobiles came along, they presented a problem for the faster traffic. Many of these bridges were replaced or redesigned on heavier-traveled roads, because drivers couldn't see over them. Some were widened to accommodate two cars, while others were preserved for historical and scenic interest. Narrow bridge signs were generally posted to warn motorists on less-traveled roads.) Shall we return to our story?

Okay! Here I come in my runaway Ford, like I'm going to a fire, totally unaware of the peril that was about to engulf me! By the time I realized my predicament, we were beyond doing anything to correct the situation. The arched bridge propelled us skyward, just like a skier going off a ski ramp, and we were soaring with the eagles in a heartbeat! Coming the opposite direction was an unsuspecting damsel in an English sports car. Her MG, or whatever it was, had been completely shielded from my view. Once airborne, I quickly lost sight of her. I'm sure we were at least twenty feet above her roofline; too high to notice what she did after we whooshed by. It's only a guess, but I'm thinking she couldn't tell, nor gave a care, what we were "sailing" in! If she noticed anything, it was the grungy undercarriage of my oily, smoking rust bucket, as we roared high overhead.

I knew she was astonished, for in the brief moment I caught a glimpse of her kisser, I could see she was clutching her steering wheel with a death grip and her mouth was so agape, she could have wrapped her lips around a walleye or a hoagie; but there wasn't any time to discuss the difference or deliberate her preferences. I shall never forget the look on her face. Her eyes were as big as saucers, steeped in horror and disbelief! It was one of those Kodak moments!

Although we cleared her with plenty of room to spare, I knew, instinctively, our fun was only in its infancy, because you know what they say? "What goes up must come down"! And boy, did we!

One thing you notice about a Ford when one gets airborne like that is they hardly make a sound. All you can hear is the beating of your heart, the filings in the oil pan, the whistling of the wind, and the humming of the engine. It is unfortunate the experience doesn't last very long!

When we resumed contact with the roadway on the opposite side of the bridge, all signs of tranquility dispersed. Every nut and bolt rang out in a thunderous kaboom, the likes of which rivaled the dropping of 500 metal trashcans filled with glass jars into a stone quarry, accompanied by a dozen Chinese gongs and a 21-gun salute!

I have no idea how my car stayed together in one piece. None of my bald tires blew out, nor did the wheel assemblies separate. Although the impact was deafening, it didn't last very long, because we were soon back up in the air again, but this time we only ascended four or five feet, versus the previous 18 to 20 we had amassed. Teddy's glasses went flying and somehow neither one of us went out through the canvas roof. I managed to hang on to the "knicker knob," and was glad to still be in "control," because no sooner had my eyeballs stopped undulating in their sockets, than they beheld a stop sign waving like a wind sock, with only a few hundred yards left to go, and we were closing on it fast!

The sight prompted me to pounce on the brake pedal, like a secretary bird stomps on a cobra. My overreaction sent our bottom-heavy "chariot" into a wild skid! Because of the wet pavement, we were sideways in less time than it would take to plaster a cop car with eggs. Unfamiliar with spins, I kept going around until the car was heading backwards. At least I had the spinning problem solved, but I'm unhappy to report I was not "out of the woods" yet, because the situation continued to deteriorate. Big "Mo" had propelled us through the intersection trunk first! I'm figuring we were still going about 40 mph, which was a slightly better set of circumstances than where I had been a few seconds previously, but looking where you are coming from is less preferable than looking where you are going! Fortunately, the oncoming traffic had stopped in both directions, which totally surprised me, but then, I suppose it shouldn't have. After all, we had been making plenty of racket long before we ever got there, so I suppose we had given everybody fair warning!

The old '51 barreled across the intersection like a black rhino on the move. I was strangling the steering wheel as if I were clutching a wad of Grover Clevelands! I suppose it was a blessing in disguise; we were still traveling backwards, and spared the observation of the final segment of our momentous journey, plus the faces of the disbelieving motorists watching an idiot take on the world. I don't doubt it was entertaining to some, but we had been at our pathway of carnage for more time than I care to mention, and were glad it would soon be over.

The final sounds we heard were a flattened stop sign on the opposite side of the road; followed by the "clang" of a street sign being leveled; the thump of a bus stop bench being taken apart, with pieces ricocheting in a thousand directions; the scrunch of a small tree; a bam, thump, and a long scratching noise on the canvas roof; all the aforementioned the result of bounding over a culvert and coming to rest underneath a towering spruce tree. The silence, mercifully, signified the conclusion of our joyride!

I glanced over at Ted, who was still fumbling around for his glasses. I could tell by his demeanor and by his pale, flushed appearance, he wasn't much impressed with my driving techniques, and was probably skeptical whether I should even be allowed to operate a pencil sharpener.

We sat there for a few moments in my smoking car, not saying anything to one another. I was replaying the experience back through my mind, feeling numb, and very fortunate that we were okay and that it was over.

I got Teddy home, but it sure was a quiet trip the rest of the day.

The property damage turned out to be a very expensive ordeal, when all was said and done; which leaves me offering a bit of parting advice. In the future, if you plan to ride a camel, make sure it has sand beneath it, not water!

The Tree Frogs of Virginia

During the time span in which our kids were growing up, we were fortunate to have gone on a number of vacations and getaways together as a family. I suppose we ran into enough adventures and thrills to write a book all by itself. This is a big country and there are so many things to see and do, and I might add, awkward and unusual situations to get into, but one of the most bizarre experiences we ever came across happened at a stopover campsite outside of Charlottesville, Virginia one summer evening.

I know that many families have the propensity to plot and plan their vacations down to within minutes of nearly every facet of their comings and goings, which is a very noble and reassuring attribute I am told, but not with this independent country boy! Not on your life! Maybe it is a by-product of my free-style childhood, but I detest having to make deadlines and adhering to a demanding schedule, when what I want to do most on a trip is relax and enjoy the adventure of the "unknown." Let the chips fall where they may is my motto. If I have to make a reservation for something that demands a reservation, I will make an exception, but I view that as merely common horse sense.

I'm not sure what year this was, but Gretchen was probably about 12 and Otto would have been 10, which would more than likely make it 1987. We found an interesting campground in our camping guide, which featured an outdoor pool. We arrived in the late afternoon, set up our tent, had something to eat, and along about seven o'clock we got into our swimwear and walked to the backside of the campground, finding the spacious swimming pool virtually unoccupied.

After a long day on the road and seeing the sights, a swim in a pool was a perfect ending of a perfect day. The water temperature was just right, and everybody interacted with each other and lounged and cavorted at great lengths. I especially liked having the whole pool to ourselves, as about an hour after we arrived poolside, everyone else left us alone. It was a very relaxing time as we watched the sun settle behind the tall hardwood forest that encompassed our peaceful setting.

As the shadows crept in upon us and dusk began to dominate the skyline, night sounds of the forest creatures native to the area commenced to introduce themselves, one by one. Most people might not notice such things, but having been an admirer of God's creation, I was attuned to His natural handiwork, which was a by-product of being raised in the woods from birth.

First was the familiar call of the evening birds, chief of which was the chatter of the mockingbirds, which are noticeably absent in the woodlands of the midwestern plains. At that time, having spent the last ten years in Iowa, I realized how much I had missed their relentless mimicking of other feathered friends in the evenings. Then I noticed the sounds of various insects, which are common to the woods; but above all those squawks and scratches I heard something so unfamiliar to me, my mind took immediate notice. It was a peeping sound.

As I treaded water, I studied the air with my ear and heard it once more, and there it was again, only from another direction. Then, another peep rang out from a different place. I was puzzled. I rolled the noises around in my mind and reasoned that our swimming pool must be surrounded by swamps or bogs or something; because I could swear they sounded like frogs, but I never knew frogs took to the trees! Within a space of a few minutes, the isolated peeps were joined by a rousing chorus of hundreds of peeps, and they seemed to be getting closer and closer all the time. Within minutes we were surrounded by them. It was beginning to look like we had stayed too long at the pool and there was no escape. It was quite an eerie feeling. It was a good thousand yards to the campsite and Mary Lou and the kids were too timid to make a break for it! This was Alfred Hitchcock's version of *The Birds*, but with an amphibian twist!

They were heading for us, all right! Millions of them! Gretchen was beginning to freak out. Never was there a living soul born with more fear and trepidation for the insect and animal world than my daughter. The sight of one harmless ant or spider would be enough to propel her into a hysterical aberration! Whenever a screaming binge descended upon my otherwise tranquil world, more times than not, it was Gretchen crossing paths with a hymenoptera or arachnid, minding its own business.

Then Mary Lou saw what was causing all the commotion. It was a tiny brown frog or toad hopping to the pool's ledge. She picked it up to show me, as she was just as interested in this strange phenomenon as I. The "beast" was only the size of a fifty-cent piece. Otto became fascinated in the calamity too, as several of the frogs jumped into the pool with us, and it was soon evident that we were going to be overrun with them. We played with them for awhile, putting them on our heads and arms, but as it grew increasingly dark, we decided that we had best call it a night and leave the frogs alone to do what frogs do at a public pool. We gathered up our towels and marched back to our tent, but Gretchen was well in the lead, as she wanted no part of the "love fest" with the tree frogs of

Virginia.

It was one of the most bizarre encounters with Mother Nature I have ever run across. I was thankful Gretchen wasn't inclined to kiss any of them, for there wasn't room in the tent for another prince.

Hoot Owl, Hoot Owl?

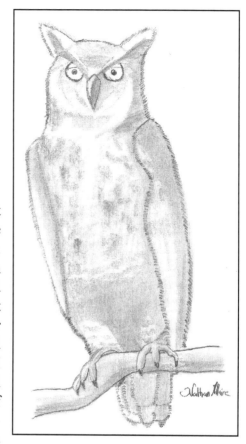

Thus far, I haven't said a whole lot about the exploits of my oldest brother. He was the first one to get in on the Getz gene pool, and from all the accounts that have whistled past my ear holes, the most creative and imaginative of us three. I would bet the farm he could write a book twice the size of anything I'll ever pen, chock-full of harebrained schemes and pranks, double the pleasure and double the fun.

I believe elder siblings have a natural and irresistible urge to tease, tantalize, and torture their younger brothers. This stems from the realization that their additional years of experience, cunning, and knowledge become uncontrollable impulses to unleash the terrors of the unknown upon your "stupid little brothers." It is the zenith of adolescence to witness your younger siblings consumed with panic and fear. Any carefully devised idea, when fully hatched, becomes a crowning achievement of youthful masculine identity. Then there is great satisfaction in knowing any grief you can dish out becomes payback for all the irritations their very existence has ever caused.

Who came up with the "hoot owl" idea, I can only hazard a guess, but I would lay odds Harvey engineered the whole thing. Here's the scuttlebutt on this box of rotten buzzard eggs.

Between our old homestead and the next-door neighbor's place was a dark, forbidding woods. A well-worn path had been etched through it that served as a shortcut out to the road. There were no streetlights nearby, so unless there happened to be a full moon, you could barely make out where the pathway went. In our later years, Reggie and I became more familiar with it and could find our way through the woods, even on the darkest of nights. However, while we were, shall we say, of a sensitive and tender age, we normally would use our front lawn to make the road, to avoid running into skunks, spooks, downed limbs, and the Bogeyman!

On the night in question, I would guess we were about six or seven. We were over at the neighborhood bully, Lonnie's place, playing hide and seek, cops and robbers, and eating our hearts out watching him play with his train set. It was past twilight when he asked us, "Shouldn't you be getting home?"

His question was right out of the blue, and it struck me funny that he would give a care whether we were safe at home, about to drown in a cesspool, or eaten alive by werewolves. I had a sneaking suspicion that he was "put up" to keeping Reggie and me busy until darkness fell, because it was unlike him to let us in his house to play with his toys.

Regardless, we knew that we were supposed to be home before it was dark, so obediently, we bid a fond farewell and started down the road for home. We hadn't gone very far when Lonnie hollered at us from his front yard, "I bet you're chicken to go through the woods!" Well, all one has to do is suggest that another kid is "chicken" or a "scaredy-cat," and the whim to prove yourself otherwise becomes a siren call!

After a long string of "I bet you're chicken" dares, we marched right into that dreaded woods like two coonhounds after a coon. It was always prudent to show a loudmouth, arrogant "spoiled brat" that you were fearless. Bogeyman, spooks, skunks, and werewolves, look out! Here we come!

We hadn't gone 50 feet down that dark, eerie path, when from high overhead came a "Hoo-hoot-hoot-hooooo, hoot-ha-hoo-hooooooooo." Our young minds didn't know what it was, because we had never heard anything like it before, but we practically ran one another over beating a retreat out of those woods. We would have lumbered halfway across the township before we would have stopped for anything! And Lonnie was stride for stride with us, shouting, "Run for it! Run for your lives! It's the Bogeyman!!!"

We kept hauling it until I thought my lungs would collapse, and I slowed down to a walk and stood still. Lonnie kept up the charade by continuing to goad us, which was always his constant pleasure; and yet, way back in the direction from where we had come, we could hear an occasional, faint "hoot-hoo-hoo" coming from the woods. The owl-like hooting went on and on and on. All the while, we were feeling trapped, as darkness was everywhere. We couldn't go forward and we weren't going back either. We were scared out of our wits and afraid to go near the woods or the road, and of course, Lonnie kept taunting and making fun of our frightened state.

Finally, after quite a long time, the hooting stopped. Reggie was crying and I was close to joining him. Suddenly, Mrs. Naylor came out of her house to see what all the commotion was about and to see where Lonnie disappeared to. She thought we had gone home and was surprised to see us. We told her that something was over in the woods and it was going to "get" us. She assured us that it was just a harmless owl and to get on home, and with that said, "Lonnie, get in the house. You boys go on home!" So, with newfound courage, we tiptoed down the road, past the woods, and across our lawn to the security of our backdoor.

Unknown to any of us, my dad had had enough owl racket for one night. He and Mom were trying to listen to some radio programs and Pop was having a difficult time concentrating. He decided to silence the owl, fetched his shotgun, and was heading up the path to put that creature out of business, when the hooting ceased.

We all found out about this, years later, when the retelling of this story and other childhood adventures came to light. We realized for the first time that had Harvey gone on a little while longer, Pop would have dusted off his "tail feathers" with buckshot!

Can you see the headlines in the newspaper the next day? "Grieving Dad Regrets Blasting Son From Oak Tree" or "Midnight Hunt Bags Rare 135-Pound Featherless Owl!" We often hear how practical jokes can backfire, but I doubt any of us knew just how close my big brother came to almost collecting a buckshot rocket into eternity one night!

Chains at 90

*F*rom personal experience, it is my belief that few males develop a firm command of common sense until they pass age 26. Some may wish to quibble over this, and lobby a few years on either side of my conclusion; but if you are old enough to have been "through the mill," you probably have enough experience to shake your head in agreement.

Fellas, have you ever said, "I can't imagine what I was thinking!" This musing is directed to one of those incidents, in my first quarter-century of life, which begs me to tell you about one of those weak moments I was involved with, because I really can't imagine *what* we were thinking!

In the summer of '61 I bought my very first car, a '51 Ford convertible. It had already seen its best days, but it was my pride and joy. It used a little oil, but I liked the idea of putting the top down, and the two "bullets" featured in the grille especially attracted my interest.

Shortly thereafter, my younger brother came home with a customized, 2-door '49 Ford coupe. It was a looker, and had new upholstery, glass-packed mufflers, dual exhaust, and lag pipes. It was all white, "nosed," and had a rebuilt flathead with a four-barrel carburetor. It was a sharper looking car than my "bomb," of course, but I was just as excited about his rod as I was with my new set of wheels.

Prior to this, we rode Lambretta motor scooters, which got us from place to place and were a lot of fun, but to have your own car was a giant step up the "food chain." This new mode of transport served us better for all the activities we wanted to be involved in, such as gallivanting, terrorizing the neighbors, peeling rubber, drag racing, backfiring mufflers, running over skunks, making "boiler-makers" on dirt roads, getting to work when we ran out of money, and going on dates. The skunk fumes were especially valuable when taking girls out, because any young lady who endured an experience like that, and accepted a second date, was either really, really interested or more desperate than was for her own good. The independence also attracted our pals like flies to a dung heap.

In the latter part of winter that year there was a huge blizzard, which blew many of the local roads shut. It took days for the road crews to get them open, as drifts were in excess of 15 to 20 feet in many places.

Naturally, we wanted to drive around and see all the "carnage," so my brother put on a new set of snow chains, and we set out to rubberneck. He stopped to pick up a couple of his classmates and take a trip through the winter wonderland. I wish I knew what it is about getting together with friends that makes the normal thinking process go out the window. How does asinine reasoning replace common horse sense so quickly? It is truly an amazing phenomenon to behold!

For instance, tire chains were designed for ice and snow in order to provide more traction. The general principle is to make it safer to get where you need to go. Now, we knew this because we had driven with Pop many times. He always preached to us the wonder-working miracle of snow chains. On our own, this knowledge proved beneficial, but somehow when we found ourselves with companions, all sound reasoning escaped our attention. Our challenge was trying to see how fast we could go and still keep the car on the road!

This Johnny Rutherford-style of driving caused one of the chain links to snap, allowing the broken link to whip slap the wheel well, which caused a resounding clacking noise, to the delight of the occupants inside the car. Instead of slowing down to minimize the noise and harm, my brother decided to ratchet up the speed to amplify the noise level! You see, noise begins when boys first start to crawl and it never stops until God silences them for good. It's a masculine trait that goes clear back to the beginning of time.

All right, now! Let us review this magic moment, shall we?

Increasing one's speed causes chain links to break and make noise. Right? Therefore, this brings great joy to the male species. Correct? Which in turn, begs for more velocity, causing more links to disassemble, increasing the racket, bringing more joy and jubilation to a giddy throng! Are you seeing a pattern here?

Thus, the next plateau of moronic conquest begs the obvious question, "I wonder how loud it will get if we floor it?" This quality is best demonstrated by shouting at the driver, "Floor it!" with cupped hands, because it is the only remaining option for communication. One person using the cupped hands method will not "cut it"; but when three people are using it at the same time, barely audible tones become recognizable to the operator, causing him to mash the accelerator pedal to the floorboard, permitting the carburetor linkage to work its magical function.

Soon, we are roaring along at 70 mph plus, which causes the one good chain to bust a link. Snap! Whack! Clacka-clacka-clacka-clacka-clack! Now, the noise intensity engulfs everyone from both sides. The stereophonic racket exceeds that for which the human eardrum was designed, causing the occupants and driver to cover both ears. This is not a recommended practice on winding, snow-covered roads, but we were giving it our best shot!

Now 90 mph is reached at intervals, as is proudly pointed out by the driver behind the wheel, who is grinning and signaling with a stabbing motion at the speedometer, using an index finger.

Neither laughter nor the rapping lag pipes is any longer discernable. The rock 'n' roll radio station had long been overtaken, due to the roar of metal bashing metal. The cacophony of busted chain links resounded off the granite cliffs, which ran parallel to the river road, sending wildlife fleeing; and I'm guessing there were a few livestock stampedes we never knew about. Still another chain link broke loose, enveloping every shred of serenity that may have remained. The only thing I ever heard that may have been louder was the gravel loader dumping crushed rock into gondola cars at the railyard.

Laughter became hysterical as we wondered what the car sounded like to passersby, oncoming cars, and the police! Police!! We forgot about the police! Fortunately, the laws of physics intervened and the left side chain completely separated and fell away. Suddenly, the chain-slapping rumble was cut in half, which came as a welcome relief. Hoarse voices and laughter subsided as we slowed for a stop sign, and for the first time in miles and miles of rough road, we welcomed the stillness. Although there was a noticeable ringing in everyone's ears, no one seemed concerned about it or anything else, but the consensus was that we had best break up the festivities and go home. In time, fond farewells were extended as the sun set in the west.

My brother and I returned home, serenaded by the frantic barking of Rex, the wonder dog, who also had the ability to appreciate barbaric racket. To put an accent on our snow sightseeing jaunt, we gave the Ford one more clattering roar up the driveway, came to a sliding halt, and parked in the backyard, where we usually kept our cars. With dreaded anticipation, we got out to assess the damage.

The unannounced rumble brought Pop to his feet and away from whatever peaceful endeavor he had been engaged in. We could see him leering out through the curtains that covered the back porch door, with his customary glare of curious disdain. These were his offspring! No doubt, our raucous re-entrance back into his life was a source of grave concern. The poor guy was accustomed to arriving home after a tough day at work to find squad cars parked in his driveway on numerous occasions, and this was long before we ever thought of cars! So, it was not out of character for him to be interested in our arrival, especially with the style of entrance we had just made. I suppose, in the back of his mind, he was awaiting another cop car with sirens wailing, to make a grand entrance into this peaceful country setting, but he presumed too much. Although by rights, we had earned the attention of the law, the only thing whistling through our ears was the west wind.

We gazed at the fender and wheel well on the left side, and were astonished to see that they had been completely eliminated; a sight we hadn't expected to see. A quick glance at the other side revealed that it was only three-fourths annihilated, but no consolation prize. We thought maybe we might have flicked off a few chips of paint, but not this! Only then did the reality of our stupidity dawn upon us. A few hours of "fun" proved very costly and foolish. It was a sad testimony.

I can't recall if my brother ever fixed it back the way it was or not, but I know he felt very badly about what he had done to his beautiful car. It was one of those times, when later on in life, you find yourself asking, "What on earth were we thinking?" I suppose, since we can't begin life at 27, we just have to make the best of the choices we deal out to ourselves.

Red Hot Maggot Snatcher

I'm not certain when this tale of woe took place, but my recollections tell me I was about twenty. I can almost hear the conversation between Uncle Emil and myself, when he mentioned a temporary night watchman job at a car dealership, where he had done some carpentry work. Basically, they needed a warm body to clean the offices, take out the trash, and keep an eye on things throughout the night until business hours began. The position was only good for two Saturday nights, until the regular janitor resumed his duties. As I was unemployed at the time, making some money seemed like a brilliant idea, so I took the job. I was delighted with the idea of being in charge of me, myself, and I, a destitute trio of money-hungry charlatans!

When I reported for work the first night, my duties were explained to me in less than five minutes. I didn't see any problems performing what they wanted me to do. In spite of the menial tasks, I was intrigued by the idea of being overseer of such a vast domain. My observation was totally delusional, but since it was rare for anyone to demonstrate confidence in me, I was swept up by the challenge of it all.

By 8:00 p.m. everyone had departed the premises and I became the "big cheese" for the next twelve hours. Although I had several chores to keep me busy, I really liked patrolling the new and used car lots most of all. My imagination propelled me far beyond reality, as I pictured myself to be an old western town marshal, ready to gun down the first miscreant that reared his ugly head. I didn't intend to plug anybody full of holes, just report suspicious-looking characters to the police, who were to drop by during the wee hours. I was told, "If people were just browsing, that was fine," but after midnight they were to "come back during the regular hours." My fantasy was a great motivator and gave purpose to my otherwise mundane situation.

In three hours I had the offices mopped, cleaned, and the trash disposed of in a dumpster, but my enthusiasm had created a problem. Because I failed to pace myself, I had nothing left to do, with seven-plus hours until I could go home. I knew if I didn't keep busy, sleep would overtake me, and I didn't want anyone to find their "trusty gun-slinging night watchman" curled up somewhere in a stupefied state, come daybreak.

So, I began to look around for things to do. The first observation that drew my attention were several black scuff marks in the hallways, which ignited the bright idea of finding a solution to getting rid of them. I scanned the utility room for something to attack this unsightly problem; meanwhile, envisioning the expressions of utter joy on managerial faces first thing Monday morning, when they beheld every single gleaming, pristine hallway floor, sparkling like gemstones amid the morning dew. I saw my "stock" going through the roof, and my fame and fortune spreading like wildfire throughout night watchman-hood!

My excitement grew as I fumbled around for a can of anything that indicated it would remove black heel marks. Then, to my quivering delight, I found a bottle of something that had the word "cleaner" on the label, and that was all my janitorial instincts needed to know. I snagged a handful of red utility rags and made a beeline in the direction of those "evil" black scuffs. I studied the situation and zeroed in on the most noticeable marks, liberally drenching them with a generous supply of my miracle solution.

What do you mean, "Read the directions!"? One has to think in order to do that! Who do you think I am—a Know-it-all? Back to the story!

I allowed the mystery juice plenty of time to soak in and do its magic. Then, I began to eradicate those ugly dark blemishes. The black scuffs disappeared, all right, but so did the tiles. I don't know what that "stuff" was, but I was glad I didn't go nuts with it! Every black spot I applied my "miracle cleaner" on began dissolving the tile and turning it into a tan fudge.

I hastily fetched a bucket of cold water and doused the floor, hoping to head off the impending disaster, and keep whatever I had on my hands from eating clear through the deck and dissolving the floor joist. It worked, but I was so filled with adrenalin and worked into a dither, by this time, I couldn't have fallen asleep unless I received a skull-crushing blow from a ball-peen hammer! Which, my managerial cohorts would have gleefully administered, if they could have seen what I was engaged in at that moment.

I soaked up the water and was relieved to find that the mop I had used hadn't dissolved before my eyes. With a putty knife, I smoothed out the injured tiles as best I could and drowned the whole area with a very generous coating of floor wax. I let it dry real good, then hauled out the floor buffer and shined that "baby" like it was the hood of a '38 Pierce-Arrow. Awhile later, I buffed the area again and it didn't look all that bad. However, the wax sealed in all the other black marks, but the scuffs I had disintegrated were no more. You'll have to trust me on that!

Needless to say, my grandiose visions of gaining hero status by turning hallways into jewel-studded "bowling alleys" were thoroughly quenched. I hatched no further impulses in that field of endeavor. I had other fish to fry!

After checking the car lots again, I took notice that it was almost 2:00 a.m. I had to find something else less destructive to engage my "trouble-shooting" impulses. Shortly after making this mental notation, I discovered a huge, disheveled pile of wooden, cardboard-covered skids out in the back parking lot. I decided that they could be busted up and disposed of, and this would keep me entertained for a long time.

Bingo! This would be the springboard into revisiting notoriety and cause my stock to spiral upward once again! I envisioned expressions of great joy sweeping over managerial heartstrings first thing Monday morning, accompanied by exultations and praise, and most of all, there would be peace in the valley.

Flailing through the "good old" utility room, I found a claw hammer and a three-foot lead pipe along the wall in the garage area. Systematically, and with a new surge of impassioned zeal, I began prying and clubbing the pallets apart.

Now, I don't know about you, but to me, sound seems to travel more intensely in the dead of night, particularly in those wee hours before dawn. Have you ever noticed this? If you stumble over a chair in broad daylight, it barely makes a sound, but when you flatten one in the dead of night, it sounds like dropping a tray of wine glasses down a stairwell.

Anyway, I can't imagine what was going through the minds of the neighbors as they were snatching their last few precious moments of shut-eye that morning. Either they were oblivious or the cornfields muffled the racket, because I was making enough commotion to rival General Grant's troops storming Lookout Mountain.

I found my new activity very stimulating. I became bright-eyed and bushy-tailed. Four bashed pallets quickly filled the dumpster to the brim, and there was nothing else to stash the debris in. I was at an impasse and had to come up with an idea to alleviate the situation; which as you may know by now, generally gives birth to some form of human misery or bewilderment!

The obvious conclusion was that I needed to reduce the size of the rubbish, and what better way to do that than consume it? For those of lesser intellectual insight, that meant FIRE!!! I would burn the wood and cardboard, and thus, eliminate my predicament. This was a no-brainer!

I located some matches and proceeded to set the trash dumpster ablaze, but first, because I was loaded down with wisdom; I removed three-quarters of the wood and paper from the bin, so that the resulting flames wouldn't leap hundreds of feet in the air and freak everybody out. This was further proof that I was "gifted" with the capacity to think things through. It was okay with me if Grant "stormed the mountain," but I didn't want *him* to burn the city to the ground!

I continued to feed the fire, while renewing my destruction of the pallets. This scenario went on until well past daybreak, when I allowed the fire to burn itself out and all the evidence was incognito.

I then retired from my night watchman duties and dutifully fled into the sparse Sunday morning traffic, and home to sweet dreams.

Sometime the next day, I overheard a news report of a trash truck (or what I have always affectionately referred to as a "maggot snatcher") catching on fire while traveling down a major highway somewhere. Evidently, an unsuspecting driver had collected a "hot" container on his rounds.

The report said, "The truck was traveling at a high rate of speed, en route to a landfill, and the breeze ripping through the cargo fanned the smoldering embers, igniting the paper and plastic contents inside the box. Motorists, following the vehicle, saw clouds of smoke billowing from the rear and frantically tried to hail the driver of his dilemma. The truck was completely destroyed before local fire companies could extinguish the blaze. Authorities were puzzled as to how something like that could happen. As there was no positive way to know where the 'hot trash' had been collected, nothing could be done except cover the loss by insurance," the news item concluded.

Naturally, I was curious about it too. To this day, I have never been certain my exploits had anything to do with the incident. I always dismissed it as just a coincidence, too remote and disconnected for me to ever know for sure. Nothing was ever mentioned about it to me, so I may only imagine any implication, and I never gave any more thought to it, than that it is an imperfect world we live in.

Giant Green Popcorn

One summer evening in 1979, Rick, a longtime friend of mine, casually asked me if I wanted to go frogging with him. It was one of those unsuspecting questions that seem to come from out of blue every once in awhile, but it changed many July to September nights for me over the next several years. Instead of pursuing peaceful sleep when bedtime rolled around, I found myself transformed from a placid homebody into a frog-hunting fanatic.

Up until that point in my life, I had enjoyed the normal things people pursued after the sun disappeared over the horizon; but the mere thought of a plate full of pan-fried frog legs was so captivating, it caused me to leave the serene company of my loving wife and family, and traipse about the local swamps and ponds, enduring some of the worst adversities Mother Nature could inflict, in order to secure this rare delicacy. And the enjoyment that Rick and I shared on these madcap outings was unmatched by anything else we did together.

I remember one incident, in particular, where we spotted a bullfrog on a muddy embankment. It was as large as a tomcat, but a dead, fallen tree blocked our way in getting close enough to spear the thing. We quietly discussed the solution, and decided to back-oar, get a running head start, and see if we could clear the sunken log and get a shot at it. We maneuvered into a starting position about 80 yards out. The plan was to row as fast as we could, then as we hit the log, I would drop my oar, grab the spear, and gig the "sucker," all in one fell swoop!

We began our assault and soon got up a full head of steam. There was just enough moonlight to make things out. We slammed into the log, which made a thunderous thud, which I was certain spooked our quarry. The canoe flew six feet into the air. I dropped the oar, grabbed the spear, and on the downward flight was surprised to see the stupid frog still perched on the bank. I held the spear out straight, and gored the frog dead center, driving it about a foot down into the soft muck. It took quite a bit more finagling, but I managed to pry the victim out of the mud and flip it overhead to my ecstatic companion, who made an end of it. It was probably one of the biggest frogs we had ever bagged, and we were so proud of what we had accomplished to get it. I only wish we could have gotten the whole thing on video. It was a Kodak moment for the ages!

Usually, I would go over to his place around twilight on the night agreed upon, garner his canoe, and hoist it atop his 1958 rusted-out, red and white Ford pickup truck, and cinch it down with straps and rope. That truck, alone, was worth the price of admission and a story in its own right. It was so rusted out from two decades of Iowa salt baths, I could look down at my feet while we were hightailing it out to the happy hunting grounds, and see the roadway whizzing past beneath. I had a canoe of my own; and I suppose I could have, just as easily, shown up at his place with my sparkling, silver canoe strapped on top of my gleaming yellow Chrysler, but it wasn't "right" for the occasion. Besides, it's a whole lot more fun to put lipstick on a pig than to gussy up a thoroughbred!

Albeit, when we would arrive at our selected destination, it was second nature to unload our boat and gear, and slither into the sultry summer night with carnage on our minds! Rick and I would paddle and navigate to the starting point, where I'd don a mosquito-mesh hat, put on a sweatshirt, clutch a three-pronged spear with one hand, and wield a 6-volt battery searchlight in the other.

My job was to scan the shoreline and reeds, looking for reflections off the frogs' bulging eyeballs, while Rick supplied a calm, steady stroke with the oar. The light would cause the frogs' eyes to glow, giving away their location, and verifying the size of the quarry. Knowing the distance between their orbs was important; because we could determine whether it was worth gliding the canoe close enough to the taker, "running it through" with the gigger. If I speared it, I would sling the catch over my shoulder, where Rick would take it off the prongs, and lop off its head with a hatchet, using a 2x4 stretched across the canoe, which served as a chopping block.

I couldn't observe any of the bloodletting going on behind me; but I received all the benefits, with each slam of the hatchet and the commentary from Rick, as to how things were proceeding. Rick was a dyed-in-the-wool outdoorsman, and a longtime hunter. He had skinned and rendered edible many a wild kill over time, and was immune and insensitive to blood, guts, and gore. He was quite familiar with finalizing the aspects of putting game out of its misery. Whereas, I was cut more out of the Gary Cooper mold of taking the hill, Rick was of the Vincent Price stripe; more suited in administering the fatal blows than contemplating how to be nice about it. For the benefit of all you squeamish non-felons, isn't frog hunting one of the most exhilarating pastimes you could ever imagine? I know the ladies in the audience just love every moment of this!

When we had our limit, we would head back to his place for the cleaning and skinning operation. On a normal night, our heads wouldn't find a pillow until well past daybreak. Sleep was easy to come by once our bodies had a chance to unwind.

However, one of the most interesting and challenging evenings

I ever spent gigging Ranis delecti, which is a fictitious Latin name I invented for the word *bullfrog*, was when I went out by myself once. On the summer night in question, I set out to investigate some new haunts I was curious about, a few miles south of where I lived. It was a very humid August night and I was having problems trying to sleep. It was just too uncomfortable, even with the fans going, but since I was up anyway, why not find something to do to pass the time?

It was then the lust of the hunt overcame me and I found myself rounding up my gear, bidding a fond farewell, and heading out into the summer night in search of "leapis panica."

I thought that some of the ponds and backwaters along the Iowa River, near the Amanas, would prove to be a great place to try my luck. I didn't take the canoe, because I couldn't imagine myself trying to maneuver it, holding a searchlight, and trying to gig frogs all at the same time. I turned off the main road onto a parking path, killed the motor and lights, and for a few moments, just sat there listening to the night sounds. It was very peaceful and still. The last crescent of the moon stood silent above the tree lines, and there was a distant hooting of an owl, which was nearly drowned out by the incessant croaking of what appeared to be thousands of frog territorial "love calls." To my good fortune, I had stumbled onto a frog jubilee. It was a jungle out there!

My heart began to race. My palms began to sweat. I had never done this on my own before. I became nervous with anticipation, rivaling a parachutist's exit from a DC-3 over Germany. This was the mother lode!

Eventually, I found the car door handle and stumbled out of the crusty brown, fake-paneled '68 Mercury station wagon, which ironically, was equally as rusted away as Rick's hemorrhaging old Ford. I rummaged around in the dark recesses of the back seat and came up with a spear, a flashlight, a bucket to put the frogs in, and insect repellent. To my chagrin, I couldn't find my knife. I searched everywhere, but soon realized that I must have left it home. Drat the luck! It was too far to go back and get it, so I determined to make the best of a bad situation and get on with the hunt.

I doused myself with a generous coating of bug spray and

headed toward the sounds that beckoned me onward. I treaded through the tall weeds and brush as quietly as I could manage, until I reached the first pool. Everywhere I pointed the light, gleaming amphibian eyeballs greeted me among the cattails and mish-mash of tall grass. This was Sutter's Mill, all right!

Something one quickly learns, when hunting frogs, is that you must pretend you are a four-ounce wood fairy, because these creatures may not have boundless intellect, but they possess a great sense of self-preservation. The slightest movement or uproar will send them packing. It's for this trait that a canoe is preferable versus going on foot. So, caution was the password, if I wanted to get close enough to use my gigger.

Patiently and stealthily, I maneuvered myself into position to thrust my weapon "home." Easing my spear to within inches of my first victim, I lunged my spear forward, bagging a large bullfrog. It kicked and fought to get away, until I elatedly freed it from the spearhead, clutching it with my right hand. Hugging the slightly steep incline of the grass-covered embankment, I made my way over to the next pair of flashing eyes, and in the same manner, scored another direct hit amidships. As usual, the unsuspecting amphibian just sat there looking goggle-eyed while I ran him through! Realizing that this couldn't go on, because I was born with only two hands; I made my way back to the car to dispose of my green friends.

As I alluded to earlier, the fastest and most humane way to put these creatures out of their misery is the chopping block. You might say it's a throwback to how things were done in jolly old England in days of yore. However, I had no means to execute my little green giants. If I let them go in their gored state, they would surely perish, which would be a useless waste of perfectly good meat. I had to think of a solution.

My eyes fell upon the bucket I had left sitting in front of the car. I had forgotten to take it with me on my foray. *That's it!* I thought. *I'll put them in a bucket of water until I can get home.* "Dennis, you are a blooming genius!" I shouted to myself.

Fetching the pail by the handle, I worked my way back toward the pond, clutching frog #1, and the spear with frog #2 still impaled on it. I carefully knelt down and dipped the gleaming vessel, allowing it to fill. I returned to the landing in front of the car, and plopped the loose frog into the bucket, which instantly proved to be a stupid move. No sooner had "green eyes" touched down, than it made one of those coveted Calaveras County leaps for liberty. I had to applaud his gallantry in the heat of battle. He recognized opportunity when it knocked!

Everything I was holding onto exploded into the air in every conceivable direction. The flashlight went one way, the bucket of water another, and the frog was off to the races! He was heading back to his harem in the weeds! Immediately, the two of us were flailing and lunging about amid the dirt, the mud, and the vegetation in pitch darkness. The only light to be had was the flashlight, which naturally, when it stopped bounding, was shining away from where we were doing battle. Getting a bead on that leaping black blur, while on my hands and knees and nearly blind, was a feat worthy of a cheetah mauling a dik-dik on the Serengeti Plain. Luckily, there was just enough illumination for me to snag that irrational beast before it made its final leap back into frog heaven, but I was on my sixteenth swooping dive at the time.

In the closing moments of the conflict, our momentum carried us down the embankment one more time! I ended up at the water's edge, half-submerged from the waist down, but still miraculously grasping my trophy prey. Undaunted, I climbed back up to the crime scene, wondering, by this juncture, whether it might not be a better idea to pay a visit to the grocery store, than to go through much more of this nonsense.

Yet, curious as to whether I had any more great ideas left in my bag of tricks concerning getting these amphibians under control, my tired mind plowed up another idea. The car! Why not the car? It was the perfect prison for "leapitus panica." I should have thought of that in the first place!

Opening the tailgate, I tossed #1 into the back of the station wagon, then pulled #2 off of the spear and let him join his wayward bedfellow. I slammed the tailgate without losing any passengers and headed back to the front lines.

Now that I had all the kinks worked out of this madcap procedure, I went on with the process of nabbing two frogs at a time, returning to the "jail" and impounding my hairless food sources, until I had gored my limit. Each time I flung a new frog into the confinement area, his gregarious cohorts went into convulsions. Each event set off a wave of violent activity in the rear of the Mercury. Frogs were leaping every which way but loose. It made me think of a giant green popcorn machine at a carnival. Where that idea popped into my mind from, I couldn't tell you.

Only when I had nabbed the final two frogs, and all their slimy playmates stopped dancing around, did I dare deposit my hunting gear in the backseat. I slid into the front seat and cranked over the engine. It was time to take these guys for a ride. I was soaked from a second baptism in the pond, when I lost my footing and tumbled down the embankment on the last go-round. By now, I had acquired enough mud to plant potatoes. The picture of that made me laugh to myself, but I had a feeling of contentment, knowing my midnight venture wasn't a waste of time.

I had a satisfied sense of well-being during the return trip home that night. One—only a true blue frogger would understand and appreciate. There is nothing comparable, nor more of an oddity, than to be driving home with a carload of bullfrogs on a hot, steamy night.

I was all worn out from the frantic night of mud wrestling, sweating like a racehorse, sitting on bloodstained seat covers, smelling of pungent frog urine, being caked with crud, and so sleepy and tired, I could barely keep the car on the road. I peered through glazed eye slits as the slightest hint of sunrise kissed the blue horizon. But it all blended together to paint a picture of peaceful satisfaction and the pride of a successful hunt.

Glory! Hallelujah! I truly wish I could have been there during the second plague of Egypt! Well, on second thought—maybe not! I guess it all depends on your perception and how much trouble you want to get into!

Measles Shot, Anyone?

Although my stint in the Air Force lasted only seven months, my tenure was not without its share of comical situations. The inescapable truth was if I got anywhere near a powder keg, somehow the lit match would end up in my hand. One blissful morning I was attempting to blend into the tall grass of my platoon and doing my best not to make ripples on the pond, but because I was still breathing, all that was necessary for catastrophe to ruin another peaceful day was for me to draw one more breath.

Flight 641 was in formation outside our barracks at Lackland AFB. We were receiving instructions from our tactical instructor about various concerns for the day. Most of the sergeant's harangue seemed to be incoherent ramblings about what a worthless bunch of neophytes we were. I was trying to absorb his fatherly advice, but most of his endless reaming had a tendency to stress even the most devoted warrior, and my weary mind was flirting with ethereal nothingness. Then like a truck horn from out of nowhere, I heard the familiar voice of Sgt. Flowers rampaging through the smoky recesses of my dull, clouded mind, "Getz! Fall out!"

Even though I was taken by surprise, my first coherent thought born from this unholy alliance kicked in. *Good night! What have I done now?*

Throughout the entire process of Basic Training, Sgt. Flowers made it abundantly clear he was nobody to fool with, and nobody with whom to display any weakness of character. Although generally good-natured, his Southern disposition rarely overlooked flaws of any degree! My pulse raced as I dutifully stepped from formation, as sprightly as my bewildered brain knew how. Snapping to attention, I boomed the exact response I knew he longed to hear. "Yes, sir!" I shouted.

In his down-home Oklahoma drawl, he commanded me to take "these girls" over to the medical building to get their measles shot. Then he proceeded to bark directions, and in the next breath declared I was in charge. He told me to get these "clowns over to the circus," took another step toward me, craned his neck, put his face a hair's breadth from my nostrils, and snarled, "You got any objections, boy?"

"No, sir!" I fired back.

For one precious, infinitesimal moment our two minds were fused, but trepidation and disbelief gripped every facet of my trembling seventeen-year-old heart. The reality of his message overwhelmed my every thought. I, Dennis Richard Getz, the lowest of the lowly (of which such epithets had been drummed into me since I had shed my last diaper), had been called upon to take command. Me, the Poster Boy for insecurity and zero confidence, had been chosen to take over, without a moment of warning, 60-plus Gung Ho recruits and march them halfway across the base, unclear of where in the blazes we were going! What possessed Sgt. Flowers to make such a decision? What virtue could he possibly have seen in me? Didn't he know I preferred obscurity to fame?

In as convincing a fashion as I could convey, Flight 641 moved out toward our objective. Proudly, I marched the column along, summoning all the commands I had been taught. I even got them to do a few cadence patterns we knew, just for show! The "forced march" was going much better than I had ever imagined, but up ahead loomed the first obstacle. It was the dreaded T-intersection, beyond which a steep, grassy ravine lay in wait. "I gotta' get this right," I said to myself. "What was that command for making right-hand turns? I should know. Why can't I think of it? Right face? No, that isn't it! Column Right? Oh, yeah! That was it!" My mind had gone blank, but thankfully, I remembered what to do just in time, because we were right at the T.

The trick to Column Right is to give the command boldly, so every soldier understands it and executes the order at the precise moment, yet ends up on the correct side of the road when we turned.

Oh, my gosh! This is big, I thought. This was a shining

moment in my military career. I wanted Sgt. Flowers to be proud of me, because doing this on the drill field was "chump change." But this was different; this was "threading a needle"! I watched the intersection like a hawk and when the forward line reached the exact spot, the moment of truth had arrived. Nervous as an expectant father and summoning all my composure, out of my mouth came the command, "By the right flank, march!"

Oh, no! Where did that come from? I had given the wrong order. In less time than it took to swat a fly on my chin, the powder keg went off! Confusion and disarray swallowed up Flight 641. Half of my unteachable neophytes, anticipating Column Right, did so. The other half obeyed what they heard, emptied the street, rumbled over the sidewalk, down into the ditch, and began trampling a well-manicured flowerbed. They crushed everything in sight, laughing like donkeys in the desert, and enjoying their jaunt through the colorful floral arrangements! My once proud unit was stumbling and falling over one another like they were in a rugby scrum. Raucous laughter consumed the advancing mob, as they smashed into rubble every remnant of plant life under the Texas sky that they could lay their boots on. I was so startled by the ugly spectacle; all I could think to do was yell, "Stop! Stop! Stop!" But my giddy squad paid no attention to my frantic orders.

Then, from the rear came a loud, hostile voice. A very familiar voice, but it sounded more like a cross between a mama grizzly and a Southern Pacific engine horn! It was none other than the charming and amiable Sgt. Flowers! "FLIGHT HALT!" All lawlessness ceased. All merriment ended, and so did my pleas for mercy.

Heads were going to roll! The grim reaper was coming for his victim! From that point, I don't remember much of anything except a crazed Oklahoma madman blistering my nostril hairs with a flurry of colorful references, mixed with spit spray. Most of the sergeant's flowery compliments I failed to grasp. Some words were entirely new to me, while most were too unclear to do me any good.

Just when I thought he was going to murder me right there in the street, someone snickered in the ranks, and in a flash that riled his britches even more. He turned and began to deal with this new flicker of insurrection. For the moment, I was glad to be out of his crosshairs and relegated to the bowels of the column, never again to command so much as a cigarette detail for the rest of my tour.

Nothing more was ever said to me about that screw-up, but I knew I had supplied 60-plus guys with a tale to be told for years to come. Sgt. Flowers took Flight 641 to the medical building, and when we arrived I was told to fall out. This time I wasn't in the dark. I had half a notion he was going to make an example out of me. I was first in line for the measles shot and I remember Sgt. Flowers telling the medic, as he grasped my puny arm, "If you got any intelligence vaccine, this airman could use a gallon."

To this day, I've never forgotten this episode with destiny, when I learned leadership has a price.

Hitchhike to Nowhere

In this day and age, you would either have to be out of your cotton-pickin' mind or in desperate straits, to attempt what my brother and I did as kids. In the summertime when school was out, and the vacation days seemed to drag by like a snail chugging through molasses, we would hitchhike rides with strangers, just for the sake of generating something to do.

Generally, Reggie and I would have a destination in mind, but more times than not, we would thumb rides just to see "who" would pick us up—often ending up in places we wouldn't otherwise venture to on our bikes. When I think of the fool-hearted ignorance of it now, and understand the danger in which we placed ourselves; I just shake my head, marveling we survived to talk about it. It's possible there weren't as many weirdos roaming around back then, but I'm more inclined to think our survival was because we were together, which proved to be our saving grace.

One of our favorite exploits, when we had fellow travelers join in, was to have the most innocent-looking "toady" thumbing, while the aggregation of giddy aspirants hid in the weeds. When an unsuspecting driver would slow down and stop, the giggling throng would rush the car and pile in the back seat like lemmings going over the brink! Very seldom did this deceitful scheme backfire, and because the ploy was so funny to us, we used the scam more often than I care to tell. Most motorists found our tactic amusing, as well, but a few times we encountered someone who took exception to our juvenile gag, which put a temporary wet blanket over our gleeful ploy, yet never deterred us.

However, one fine day, we met our Waterloo. If my recollection is right, I believe we never fancied "hitchhiking to nowhere" ever again. Sometimes divine providence intervenes when one least expects it, and it can be the best thing, when ignorant ambitions could come back to bite you. Due to the fact we always made our way back home; we developed a smug attitude about hitching rides with total strangers.

On the day in question, we decided to thumb our way into Doylestown, which was a good ten miles from Solebury, as the crow flies. When we arrived, Reggie and I accomplished little more than clutter up the stores and climb the statues in the city park, as we didn't have any money or any real plans. We had been in town many times with Mom and Pop, but this was "big stuff," getting there on our own. By mid-afternoon we grew tired of our adventure and had done all that was of interest to us, so we decided to hitchhike our way home. Besides, we were getting hungry and knew it was getting late. We thought it a good idea to be home when the supper dishes were passed around.

When we got out to the main highway, not one soul took pity

on us. We never did get a ride. It took us hours to finally drag our sorry carcasses up the driveway and into the homestead. It was getting close to dark by the time we reached the backdoor, and what awaited us was not a very welcome reception.

To be honest, we really didn't know what to expect, but Pop was absolutely furious, probably more concerned than mad. He wanted to know where we had been and mentioned that he was about to call the police. We confessed our crime, but to our utter surprise, we didn't get our rear ends lambasted or our heads beat in, which was the usual reward for such offenses. Nonetheless, we were dealt a couple of backhands, and went to bed without so much as a stale cracker to munch on. We were told not to try a stunt like that again.

I don't know whether it was the reprimand or the slugs across the "bean" that deterred us from testing our hitchhiking prowess like that again. I think we were so bushed from all the walking we did, we instinctively knew another adventure of that type was not as much fun as our curious minds made it out to be. But when you are ten, it is a good lesson to learn!

Sawmill Campgrounds

Anniversaries and birthdays seldom require a reminder. Commonplace things blend into our daily routines, but rare occurrences, even misfortunate happenings, leave an indelible impression on us, especially the date they transpired. August 17, 1955 is one such date for me.

The reason? Hurricane Donna roared through Eastern Pennsylvania the very next day, bringing one of the worse floods ever to visit the Delaware River Valley. The heavy rains that accompanied the storm ran off the parched earth, caused millions of dollars in damage, and cost many their lives from the flash flooding of swollen streams.

There was a vacant field west of our home, where for years Uncle Emil had established a sawmill; which produced lumber from trees salvaged off of cleared land, and in turn were used for his construction projects. Logs were stored at the mill site, cured, and made into whatever wood materials he needed.

It was not uncommon to hear the old sawmill running from time to time, but when work was finished, everyone went home. It was a great haunt for my younger brother and me. We loved to walk the logs, play in the sawdust piles, and explore all the neat places to hide. I wouldn't describe the place as a "magnet." We were into too many other avenues of pursuit and curiosity for it to be that. The sawmill was just one more stopping off point on our itinerary of looking for trouble.

A month previous to the hurricane, we noticed a small house trailer parked over at the mill. Quite naturally, its presence aroused our interest, which demanded a full investigation. You see, Solebury was a small country town and anything going on "forced" us to check it out, or in other words, we would stick our noses in where they didn't belong!

However, let me be very clear about this snooping business, right here and now. Our pop instilled in our thinking processes a healthy respect for other people's property. "The right to own property is a cornerstone of freedom. You kids leave my stuff alone and leave other people's things alone. If it doesn't belong to you, keep your hands off of it!" I would often hear him say. But he never said anything about how to deal with curiosity, so we, quite naturally, talked ourselves into a frenzy over that trailer.

The first mistake was noticing it in the first place. We wondered who put it there. Next, we tortured ourselves as to whether or not anybody lived in it, which necessitated spying on it for quite awhile. We thought all kinds of things, like maybe it belonged to a gangster or a hermit. When we convinced ourselves not a creature was stirring, not even a mouse; the next step was to put our crummy hands on the door handle. This produced the knowledge that the trailer wasn't locked. If it wasn't locked, then there couldn't be anything important inside. This brought us to the final stage in our conspiracy, which became decision time for us. Should we leave other people's property alone or yield to temptation? We yielded!

Now the wheels really began to turn. We were turning out schemes faster than our fantasies could encompass them. Thoughts ran wild! If it was abandoned, and nobody wanted it, wasn't there something about "Finders, Keepers; Losers, Weepers"? Yeah! Property Rights! Pop was a blooming genius! The place was ours for the taking. We always wanted a clubhouse of our very own!

Once inside, we noticed there was a table with benches, an icebox that had goodies in it, canned goods, tons of artistic magazines, along with all sorts of unusual clothing. We were filled with more questions than we had answers for. What would Uncle Emil need a place like this for, when he already had his own home? If the trailer didn't belong to him, whose was it? Hey, maybe it was a gangster hideout! Maybe it belonged to a deranged screwball! That would explain the wacky duds! If this was a hideout of a bank robber, we could nab him and collect the reward! Reward? Maybe he had the loot stashed away somewhere! If we found it, we'd be rich and the crook would be in jail, but our searching didn't turn up so much as a brass button or two. There were no moneybags to be had. Our only conclusion was that the trailer had been ditched and the crooks never made it back to their lair.

For days we visited and observed the "hideout," but not a soul ever darkened the door.

Toupee Olé!

My father, with all due respect, was as bald as a summer onion and his brother Frank didn't fare much better. Consequently, during my growing up years, I was haunted with the fear I would end up resembling my forebears. Imagine how ecstatic I was when I reached my nineteenth birthday and noticed I still had a myriad of wavy locks.

In high school I groomed my Frankie Avalon pompadour like it belonged to some endangered species of mohair goat, thinking glimpses of my waves caused every dame in town to get weak-kneed. I had no intentions of my scalp becoming a landing strip for deer flies, and followed all the sound advice that came my way, such as: "Stay away from hair oil and greasy pomades. Don't use harsh shampoos. Wash your hair with Ivory soap and rinse thoroughly!"

Then one day I happened to catch a glimpse of myself in a mirror and guess what I observed? That's right, kemosabe! I detected the first signs of a receding hairline. My heart sank. *Oh, no!* I thought. *How can this be? I'm beginning to lose my hair!*

As we all know, youth is a fleeting thing and as time marched on, I slowly began to take on more and more similarities to my ancestry. The traumatic impact of losing my cranial glory bothered me very much, so I finally resolved to do something to alter the course on which the gene pool was pulling me. Taking the bull by the horns and marching against the odds, I investigated the cost of restoration methods, hairpieces, and transplants, but it all came down to simple economics, which was money. I saw an ad in the paper and inquired about a hairpiece, whereby a salesman appeared at my door one evening and explained a host of remedies for my Phil Silvers' resemblance. When all the options were explained to me, I settled for an $800 "rat's nest," which I thought was the most frugal solution.

The authentic-looking fur piece was attached to my scalp, using two-sided tape, guaranteed to withstand gale force winds, drenching rainstorms, and all other elements Mother Nature might send my way. Furthermore, I was assured it wouldn't fade, no one could tell I was carpeted, and I could go swimming in a cement mixer and it would stay on.

The very next week, after acquiring my new toupee, I attended a family picnic at my brother's place in Buckingham, Pennsylvania. It was a chance to flaunt my new youthful look and test the reaction of the next of kin. Featured activities at the get-together were croquet, quoits, badminton, and a huge above-ground pool. My hairpiece passed all the activity tests with flying colors, and nobody seemed to notice the change in me; or if they did, figured it best to avoid asking questions, which left the swimming pool as the final obstacle on my itinerary.

Donning my trunks and brimming with confidence, I ascended the diving platform for takeoff and plunged headfirst into the glimmering aquifer, emerging from the other side. When I broke surface, the air was filled with hysterical laughter and shrieking young girls, totally beside themselves. At the same time, I noticed a dark, hairy blob floating near the center of the pool, quivering in the sunlight, and looking every inch like a bludgeoned muskrat.

I frantically searched my scalp for my furry friend, but it was gone. The much-ballyhooed $800 investment that had been triumphantly trumpeted *won't come off* and *nobody will ever notice!* was bobbing up and down on the waves, leaving me looking for a hole to crawl into. This was *not* the impression I intended to leave with my family concerning "a more youthful me." The jig was up!

Wisecracks flowed abundantly. At least now, everyone could comment about my sham and freely express what they had been thinking to themselves all along. After facing reality and accepting the humor of the situation, my hairpiece seemed more natural where it was than glued to the top of my noggin. Although my embarrassment was difficult to swallow, I spent the rest of the day just being myself and lapping up the attention my rat's nest had created. All the same, I continued wearing my "rug" for special events for the next several years; because, for one, I had shelled out a lot of loot for that trapping, and at age 33, there was no going back as I clung to the last vestiges of youth, and it really was an improvement.

In 1976, when I moved to Cedar Rapids, one of the first things I did was join the Harmony Hawks Barbershop Chorus in that fair city, and since nobody knew me, I decided to continue my hairpiece charade. For close to ten years I grew relatively certain none of the chorus members suspected that I wore a toupee. At least, I never heard any comments to lead me to suspect otherwise.

I kept it a closely-guarded secret and did my best to avoid sharing sleeping quarters when the chorus traveled to competitions. I even used extra tapes to keep the "beast" in place during dress rehearsals, stage shows, costume changes, and every other situation that might arouse suspicion. Keeping it hush-hush was nothing short of a Houdini trick, to be sure.

Unfortunately, because time keeps moving on, a problem arose which I hadn't figured on. I began to notice my graying sideburns getting whiter and clashing with the guaranteed never-to-fade hairpiece. To conceal the problem, I came up with a brilliant idea of using brown shoe polish to blend in the differences, and it worked well for a long time, but deep down inside, I began to war against the phoniness of the guessing game. I not only had to carry on the deceit with the guys in the chorus, but with every other social circumstance in which I found myself. Eventually, I grew more frustrated with the constant hassle of dealing in deception; yet, I couldn't muster up the courage to go "cold turkey," shed the rug, and face my accusers, because in the back of my mind, the embarrassing experience in Buckingham still loomed large.

I had really boxed myself into a corner and the quandary of dealing with the situation was pressing in on me. The dam broke one night, several weeks later, while the chorus was busy rehearsing for our annual Barbershop Show at the Paramount Theatre in C.R. We were putting the final touches on the show package of songs, with stage lighting and all the technical things involved with putting on a "Broadway show." Everyone was growing weary of the arduous striving for musical perfection, the demands on our tired minds, and relentlessly standing on the risers. We all wanted to go home and call it "good," but the 'powers that be' held us prisoners. The chorus had reached the point of working on the closing number of the show, and I happened to be in the second row middle stage.

At one place in the number, the chorus was to do an arm spread, whereby one half of the chorus would fling their arms and torsos out to the right, while the other half would do likewise to the left. We were to do the exact same thing during the final chord of the song, giving the audience a big crescendo with the big visual effect. Perhaps it was emotional fatigue, coupled with the intensity of the moment that prompted me to do it, but when we hit the grand finale for "the eleventy-ninth time," my resolve gave way to impulse. I grabbed my toupee, ripped it off my head, and gave it a mighty heave out over the front row of merry makers. I couldn't believe I had done it and thought to myself, *Now what, you big dummy?*

As if sprouting wings, "it" sailed over the director's head and fluttered like a wounded quail, coming to rest near the footlights. In its final moments of life, "it" skidded to a halt, lying center stage in all its glory; while the chorus held their spread, with all eyes transfixed on the mysterious object, as the final chord fell apart. The entire event blossomed and died, just as if it had been choreographed solely for this one purpose.

The last note perished as if there had been an assassination, and for a few moments, everyone froze in disbelief, wondering, "What in the world was that?" Every weary soul had been so focused on getting the final notes right, the last thing anyone expected was to see a flying muskrat steal the show! Stone cold silence lingered, as if expecting a second hairy missile to appear, and no one moved or breathed for the longest time, anticipating such an event. Then, behind me, someone recognized my transformation and as if on cue, the entire chorus grasped the same conclusion of what had just taken place and broke into uncontrolled riotous laughter.

I had no idea my hairless head would strike so many men with so much levity, or I would have flipped my lid a long time before that! It must have been ten minutes before anyone could gain composure. Each time the director tried another stanza, someone would burst out laughing, and the attempt would disintegrate. There were suggestions to keep the rug toss in as part of the act, but the idea never got any traction. It took resolve, and the director finally finished the rehearsal that night, but for years guys brought the subject up so they could revisit it again. Some told me that they would be driving down the road or be standing in line, when the visual replay would surface out of the blue and break them up. My mind still pictures the flight of that toupee, and the brevity of that ill-fated moment lives on for me too.

I never wore my "rug" after that, and have wisely accepted myself for who I am, relieved to have put my vanity behind me. I still keep the hairpiece in the top drawer of my bedroom dresser as a reminder of that humorous and difficult time in my life, and will always fondly refer to that night at the Paramount as Toupee Olé!

Feet Like a Duck

The Christmas season is the best time for giving, but it presents a major problem which can often befuddle the male giver. In my case, I can usually figure out what to get everybody else on my list, but when it comes to the Mrs., I normally end up in a materialistic wasteland, dismayed, hassled, and half out of my mind. Now, I can't speak for anyone else in the paternal loop, because most guys, I believe, try to be practical and stick to the basics. Either that, or they can't think outside the box under any circumstance, and tragically show up on Christmas morning with a moose head wrapped in blue tin foil, or something along the lines of a ten-gallon jug of Polish dill pickles. Whereby, the baffled spouse just bats her grateful eyes and says thanks, vowing to put her hints in writing next time, bypassing his gut feelings.

Where I run into trouble is trying to combine practicality with uniqueness, while tossing in usefulness, eye appeal, and cost. The cost part becomes my Achilles heel; in that I'd like to think I could afford to pay for it, while not giving her the impression that my gift is a bribe!

So it was, one Christmas, I found myself in one of those highbrow shopping centers in search of a pair of shoes for my wife. With an idea like that, I was just asking for trouble, but I figured I had "practical," "original," "useful," and "unique" pretty well-covered. It was "price" and "eye appeal" I was leery about. Those two loomed on the battlefield like dragons in chain mail, but I plunged past the lingerie, purses, and perfume, all the same, because I had shoes on my masculine mind and I was on a mission.

There I was, aimlessly wandering around in a women's shoe department before I knew what hit me. Although I was trying to give the pretense that I was right at home, let me be clear, brother, this is not a great place for guys to hang out, even if you understand the nature of the beast. When a man is looking for a pair of shoes, it generally takes about three minutes flat! That's because most guys don't care to haggle over size, color, or any other variable. We pretty much have the thing figured out before we ever turn the engine over to make the trip.

Mostly, we get what we bought seven years ago, when we bought our last pair, and nine times out of ten, the only reason we splurge on another pair can be traced to a disaster or emergency of one kind or another. For me, it takes something like my dog chewing one in half, or the sole holes are letting water in, and my socks keep getting wet. Then, there is the "I don't know where I left them" excuse, which is an entirely different can of worms. Guys can pinball and mumble all day long, but it won't do much good than to dig a bigger hole, because the question "How could you lose your shoes?" always comes up. A lot of times, men will buy a new pair only because the flopping soles make noise when they walk into church and sit down. The commotion draws attention, and the one thing that puts the "little lady" in a killing mood is to have other people staring at her because of you. Then, there is the old standby "They flew off the roof of the car on the way home." Rarely do men even try to explain mishaps like this, preferring instead to act dumb, which most times carries the day in style.

Anyway, once inside the shoe store, it took some doing, because I had to take a bit more time making a selection out of respect for all the scrutiny my wife gives to the process, but my purchase took four minutes total. I left the store with a "lovely" pair of genuine Hungarian, low-heeled burgundy gems. They were the envy of every high-class gal one would find prancing down The Great White Way! I was certain that I was going to "score big" come Christmas morning. I just knew Mary Lou would take one look at those fabulous hoof trappings and squeal with delight and wonderment, totally amazed that a numb-numb like me possessed such practicality and thoughtfulness.

Weeks passed and the anticipation grew. A few days before Christmas, I took one more admiring gaze at her surprise gift, before I wrapped them in the most discriminating paper I could lay my hands on. When I affixed a colorful bow, I reassured myself of what a "hero" I would soon be.

Then came the Christmas morning celebration with all the family. True to form, it was a gift-opening free for all! When the Mrs. opened her "practical," "original," "useful," "neat-looking," and "inexpensive" pair of imported dress shoes, she was ecstatic, but I had that sixth sense there was an air of concern in the dark recesses of her calculating mind.

You see, my dear wife was raised on a dairy farm, and on a dairy farm it was a common activity for country kids to go without shoes all summer. While that may have been fun, there were consequences from such behavior, most noticeably, the tendency to develop flat feet. That translates into having wide pedals, which for a girl means, when you grow up and venture into shoe stores to get a pair of shoes, guess what? They don't make shoes to fit the flippers of a gray seal!

Typical of most married men in this age or any other, I was not aware of all the quirks my wife possessed, and in this instance, I did not realize she bought all her shoes at specialty shops. To make a long story short, there I was, the day after Christmas, hightailing it back to the mall, returning the footwear my wife had no earthly use for, all because I wanted to be clever and creative.

I no sooner stepped into the overcrowded main entrance, when some anxious-looking female from Channel 9 News shoved a microphone under my nose and excitedly asked, "Good morning, sir! Are you here to return a gift?"

I was caught completely off-guard. My mind was nearly a total blank and the last thing I expected was to undergo an oral exam about my Christmas-buying mannerisms. I noticed a cameraman with a bank of lights, who wasted no time wading in on the confrontation before him. He quickly joined the reporter and seemed eager to capture this historic moment for all posterity.

My reply came swiftly, "Yes, I'm returning a pair of shoes!"

"For yourself?" the inquisitive wench fired back.

In a matter-of-fact response, I said, "No! They're my wife's. She has feet like a duck!"

My unabashed comment caused her face to light up like a neon sign on a dark night. She leaned closer to me and inquired once again, beaming like an expectant mother, "What did you say, sir?" No doubt, her feminine instincts were wrapping their tentacles around the possibility she had stumbled onto a literary gold mine of monumental masculine suicide in the raw!

I said louder, so she couldn't miss it, as I suspected she was hard of hearing, "She has feet like a duck!!!"

With the suddenness with which they had appeared, the lights, camera, and the info-babe vanished from view faster than a flash. So, I completely dismissed everything concerning what had just taken place, the incident evaporated from my mind like a truck horn on a foggy morning, and I went about my business of exchanging the shoes.

That night, they must have run my interview on the evening news, because when I showed up for work the next day, dozens of people began asking me questions like, "Need a good lawyer? Where did you sleep last night? Can I see the lumps where she bashed in your skull? Was there room on the couch for the dog?" along with other wisecracks such as that.

Honestly, I never saw the clip on TV and didn't know what they were talking about, but I would have given anything to have partaken. Both of us got a kick out of all the ribbing, because Mary

Lou was asked similar questions. We wished we could have seen what everybody got such a charge from, because it must have been a lark.

I know one thing for certain. I'll never forget the astonished look on that reporter's face as long as I live! She looked like I had just given her the combination to the Bank of England. I guess she knew a good story when it landed in her lap! As for me, I always stick to the basics, anymore, when it comes to Christmas presents, and price is never the object!

Turkey Tails

Late in my dating experience, I stumbled upon the idea of creating a "magical moment" with a certain young lady, the identity of whom shall remain a secret. That mystical brainstorm is of no consequence these days; because our fragile relationship went "in the tank" a short time afterwards, which only goes to show that there wasn't anything mystical or magical in the plan.

My inspiration centered on taking my mystery date to a very exclusive dining establishment. In its heyday, this particular historical colonial hotel, livery, and stagecoach stop was a strategic layover for weary travelers in the days of yore. It was located on the Old Easton Highway, thirty miles north of Philadelphia. Although my memory fails me in recalling the name of this high-class tourist trap, I don't doubt George Washington may have slept there, as they like to say; but make no mistake about it, dear hearts, no hamburger joint, this! I could have taken her and her entire family to the Dairy Queen sixty times for the same money as this adventure.

It was my first Thanksgiving away from home and I wanted the day to be special, so I made reservations, which was a requirement of restaurants of this caliber. Giving my name made me feel influential, because I once worked as a dishwasher at one of these places when I was a kid. Leaving reservations is something the "muckety-mucks" perform when frequenting such eateries. What I was trying to prove could only be blamed on youthful misinterpretation of reality. I think most would prefer to call it naivete!

I had spent the better part of the afternoon washing and waxing my yellow Corvair in preparation for the event, later dressing in the only suit I owned. Dutifully, I drove over and picked up what's-her-name. She was decked out in attire suitable for a box seat at the

Kentucky Derby. Uneventfully, we arrived in plenty of time for our rendezvous with destiny.

When we entered the palatial landmark, we were royally greeted and escorted to our table by a sharp-looking hostess. She seated us at a cozy, nook-like table, next to a red-curtained window—complete with candlelight, red-and-white-checkered tablecloth, and enough silverware to bury a good-sized Shetland pony. Wherever we cast our eyes, the decor spoke of elegance, luxury, and antiquity. In the deep recesses of my mind, thoughts of whether I might be in over my head spearheaded a notion to make tracks for the Dairy Queen, but it was too late to jump ship, and besides, we were "well out to sea" and the sharks were swirlin'!

None of this material splendor mattered, because as we will soon see, my "knight in shining armor" routine was about to come to a screeching halt. Enter stage right, a delightful, well-dressed waitress, who introduced herself and made us feel welcome. She laid out our menus, made several trips to and fro, supplying us with rolls and butter, along with all the complimentary appetizers known to the civilized world. While all that preparation was taking place, we considered our dining choices and drank in our lush surroundings.

Allow me to interrupt your train of thought for a moment. For we must leave this romantic setting of "young love in bloom," and interject a very strange, but vital fact of life. During my growing up days, I developed a fancy for turkey tails.

"What," you may be asking yourself, "did you say?"

Well, allow me to explain. Whenever I found myself at a feast where turkey was served, I always asked "dibs" on the turkey's tail. That is the part that goes over the fence last! In most situations, that particular piece of the bird was either tossed out with the garbage or dogs would end up wolfing it down. Most turkey connoisseurs never gave that worthless piece of gristle one thought beyond, "Oh! Doesn't that make the turkey look grand?" Everyone I ever knew would just stare at it and harbor perverse thoughts! Certainly, no self-respecting mortal would eat one. The way I see it, a guy is entitled to at least one vice in this life and it may as well be turkey butts! You could do worse! Now, back to our impassioned couple. As the mysterious damsel and I were ordering our entrees, and because I didn't wish anyone to overhear my strange request, I leaned over to the charming waitress and whispered my odd desire in her ear. "Would you ask the chef if he has a couple of turkey tails lying around, to include one with my dinner?"

Grinning sheepishly, the astonished waitress nodded, but I sensed she didn't take me seriously and probably wasn't certain if my elevator went to the top floor, so I added, "The chef probably heaves them in the trash. Please ask the cook to toss a few on my plate." That did it! I could see in her demeanor and in the dazzled gleam of her eyes, that she was processing my request and thinking to herself, "Where does this 'meathead' think he is, the Salvation Army Homeless Shelter?"

Nonetheless, she pursed her lips, and withdrew without saying another word. I never really thought about it at the time, but I'll bet anything she just couldn't wait to get out of earshot and behind closed doors to let loose her pent-up, spit-spraying guffaw, and share our encounter with the chef.

Having overcome this giant hurdle, my date and I settled down to a round of meaningless conversation. Across from us, a very large family was seated around a huge table in the middle of the room. They were engaged in the process of waiting for their orders to arrive. Shortly, a busboy wheeled out a cart loaded down with all their selections, and two waitresses were soon busy sorting out their choices. They served their patrons as quickly as they could, and would often bend down and take full plates from a bottom shelf. We were captivated with the entire goings-on and marveled that the two girls seemed to know which of the twelve guests got what.

About this time, a barmaid tried to sneak past with a large tray of mixed drinks raised high over her head. Precisely as she reached the middle of the table and had turned to squeeze by, one serving waitress rose up and caught the drink tray dead center with the top of her head, catapulting the entire menagerie skyward. Helplessly pinned against the red curtains, the tray of booze rained down upon me like liquid fireworks. I was quickly drenched with whiskey, draft beer, martinis, and who knows what? The baptism only took a moment or two. No one else received a single drop. Good thing I wasn't an alcoholic or I could have licked myself into a frenzy in no time!

Everyone became apologetic and concerned with the unfortunate situation. I was given a towel to dry myself, and in short order, the owner came to our table, offering his apologies and concern. In the back of his mind he was probably thinking I might be the son of a bank president or some other underling, just itching to make his life miserable over something of this magnitude.

Although I was inconvenienced and uncomfortable, I had no designs on giving them any grief. In fact, I wanted to stay, but the owner insisted I go home and change. He offered to hold our dinners until I returned and promised to send my suit to the dry cleaners. They even gave us gift certificates for two complimentary dinners at a future time, and to top it off, they insisted our evening's fare was "on the house."

I never did find out how much the "peace offering" totaled, but I kept the fifty bucks I had expected to spend, which was much to my liking.

The capstone of the evening was when I finally returned in my new attire, and my date and I had recaptured our composure, vowing to salvage our evening gone awry; out of the swinging doors of the kitchen appeared the chef, along with a large entourage of staff. They were all beaming radiantly from ear to ear, bringing our long-awaited meals with all the fanfare accorded to royalty.

When my plate was placed before me, I could not believe my eyes! There, right under my nose, were, count 'em!!! Eight turkey butts!!! Not one! Not two! Not five! But eight golden brown, fat-laden turkey butts!!! Talk about overkill! Not one speck of white meat. No dark meat. Only turkey tails lying atop one scoop of mashed potatoes, 26 peas, a dash of cranberry sauce, one large glob of stuffing, and a dollop of gravy. I do believe my astonishment exceeded that of my formerly dumbfounded waitress, who was among the foremost grin-bearers, looking on at our happy gathering. I was unable to speak a word. Every crevice of my mind was completely flabbergasted in disbelief! Upon receiving my swine slop, all I could manage was a politely restrained "Thank you."

The proud chef, standing tall while stroking his elongated mustache, responded with, "I hope everything is satisfactory, sir! If there is anything else we can do, don't hesitate to ask."

Trust me. I didn't dare say another word. How could I? After all they did to make good my misfortune, humbleness seemed the only honorable response. As I glanced over at what's-her-name's bountiful, picturesque platter, I realized that sometimes it is best to keep silent when one is dining out.

Yes, it is true. I consumed them all! And, all the while, I pretended that it was one of the most delectable dining experiences of my life, thankful at least, that it was "on the house." Oh, and one final thought. To this day, when eating out, I have never requested anything more than "Do you have catsup?"

What's in Your Lunch Bag, Sonny?

Forgetfulness has been a chink in my character since the earliest days of my existence. I was always leaving things out in the rain, down at the playground, and over at somebody's house. I probably misplaced everything a kid could lay his mitts on, including some of Pop's prize tools. I will never know the number of things that ended up in someone else's possession, due to my absent-minded tendencies. In reality, we are all guilty of misplacing stuff, but I believe my forgetfulness caused me more problems than I could ever count.

My mother generally packed a lunch for me when I attended elementary school, but true to my nature, I managed to leave nearly every one of them somewhere, which the flies, mice, and mold spores dined on other than me. What didn't help matters was there never seemed to be any consistency with the whole operation. When Mom did pack a lunch for me, my mind was usually elsewhere when I exited the back door! Once or twice a year, I might have some money to buy a cup of soup from the soup lady, Mrs. Walters, but normally I spent my lunch hours watching my classmates munching on their goodies, hoping some bleeding heart might take pity on me, and hand off a tidbit they didn't want.

What seemed strange to me, most of my school chums were wolfing down cuisine totally foreign to my backwoods existence, but I never refused anything they forked over. I guess when you are starving to death half the time; there's no sense "gettin' fussy"! Besides, it wasn't every day I could eat duck eggs, smoked carp, apricot pie, and shrimp salad sandwiches. I tell you, those classmates of mine came from families steeped in weird and unconventional chow halls! Half of them must have been related to Howard Hughes, because I rarely rose above yellow mustard, Spam, and Sunbeam bread, even on a good day!

Getting back to this forgetfulness trait I was going on about, I have concluded the root cause of my trouble was attributed to the fact I had a mind focused on too many thoughts at once, which featured weekly thumpings, surviving death threats, and doing jail time. Consequently, my vacillating state made it easy to neglect the obvious, and zero in on the meaningless. Some "shrinks" would call it being lame-brained, but I never found time to argue, as I was always on the run.

When I graduated to the middle grades, I took it upon myself to throw my own lunches together, but the bad thing about that was I was forced to ride the school bus. Many times I would arrive at school only to discover I had forgotten to make anything or I had left it somewhere. It was so frustrating knowing I had "done it again"! All it took was one minor distraction, and I realized it was going to be "sponge time" again, come noon. In a word, my situation had grown pathetic!

In high school I went hungry most of the time, and had become too embarrassed to scrounge like I did in grade school. I figured it was my fault, anyway, and best to take my medicine like a man. Kids would offer me ghastly stuff they didn't want, like egg salad and cream cheese sandwiches, orange rind marmalade on pumpernickel, or sardines, pickle relish, and ketchup on soda biscuits; all of which would gag a famished hyena. I usually ate their offerings rather than watch them chuck them in a trashcan. Once in awhile, I had a few cents to get something at the cafeteria, but I usually saved my money, as I rarely had any.

With nobody to look out for me at home, my forgetfulness carried over into other responsibilities, like gym class outfits, homework, library books, and anything else you could name. No matter how much I tried to organize myself, I never seemed to get a handle on my problem enough to avoid turmoil and complications at school. One day, though, my empty-headedness produced one of the most hilarious situations I ever got myself into, which to this day, remains a source of laughter.

I was sitting on the risers in the gym, with a group of kids, enjoying one of those rare times I had my own brown bag. Among my treasures were a hard-boiled egg, tuna fish sandwiches, and some gingersnap cookies. I was accustomed to cracking eggs on my knee to break the shell, but on impulse, I chose to bust it over an underclassman's head. I don't remember the kid's name now, but to my stunned surprise, the raw egg disintegrated, sending a slimy, gushy spray of egg guts down his neck and inside his shirt.

It happened so fast I was rendered speechless, while the recipient became instantly much more animated. Let me tell you, I would describe my victim's reaction to be similar to that of a stallion being stung by a nest of hornets. I wasn't certain whether I was going to live or die; I did try my luck at apologizing, but busting raw eggs over somebody's head is a tough road to go, if you are seeking endearment from your fellow man!

From then on, the practice of cracking eggs over other people's heads fell into disfavor, particularly among the BBB crowd, better known as the Brotherhood of Brown Baggers. As for me, I came to the conclusion that, forgetting my lunch three days out of five, and wandering aimlessly around campus during lunch hour were blessings in disguise, giving way to a leaner, healthier lifestyle.

It wasn't until I entered the military that I began to gain control of my problem. The regimented requirements turned out to be a godsend, because the responsibilities forced upon me caused me to think more about others, who were relying on me for their survival. That lesson made the difference and I realized that forgetting things was just a stage I had to work my way through; and as for breaking hard-boiled eggs, I began to use countertops!

The Lambertville Cardinals

The chain of events to follow happened when I was right in the middle of the muddle-headed age of fourteen, and wouldn't have taken place, had I not yielded to one silly momentary impulse, which landed me in more hot water than I ever imagined. The siren song that got the mayhem started took place on a humid August afternoon in 1956. I had just assembled my Cardinal baseball uniform and was peddling to a game, on my bicycle, in Lambertville, New Jersey. It was a leisurely 45-minute downhill ride. The game wasn't for another four hours, and I was anxious about getting there on time. The driving force was the coach of the Cardinals, a man I highly admired and respected, because earlier that spring he had made a special trip up to my house in Solebury, expressing hope that I would play center field for him in the Babe Ruth League again.

I couldn't hit worth a hoot, but I had played seven games in the outfield for the Cardinals the previous year, and because I wrecked my bike, I had no way to get to the rest of the games that summer and had to quit. The coach said he liked my hustle and would work with me to improve my offensive skills. Rarely did anyone offer such encouragement, and for him to go to all the trouble to find out where I lived, just to see if I would play for him, was an honor I couldn't repay. Therefore, it became very important that I make it to every practice and game, whatever the cost or effort on my part. As I mentioned, it was a very steamy afternoon, and as I peddled out of town, the thought occurred to me how nice it would be to take a quick swim. There were no public pools, but I did have permission to swim at a lady's house I did occasional lawn work for; however, there was a drawback. I was on the wrong side of town. Even if I rode back to the owner's place and asked permission, there was no guarantee I could go swimming. First, I was all by myself and she wouldn't want me swimming alone; secondly, she would more than likely be using the pool, which meant it would be a waste of time to bother asking. Well, up jumped the devil!

I had a choice to make! From where I was, I could walk through a cornfield, down a wooded hillside, and I'd be at the pool in minutes. And, since all I wanted to do was take a quick dip; what harm could it possibly do? So, I hid my bike and headed for the swimming pool. When I arrived, I discovered no one was about. I worked my way through the brush, to the blue oval pool at the edge of the clearing, surrounded by tall hardwoods and a well-kept lawn. A winding grassy path led up to the house, a quarter-mile up the hill, concealed by a dense thicket.

I took a moment to listen for voices, and hearing none, disrobed and dove in the water. Boy! A quick dip was all I needed. It felt so cool and invigorating, as moments before I had been wringing with sweat. However, my joy was short-lived. I had no more than surfaced, when I heard faint laughter coming from the direction of the house. I listened, and sure enough, human voices were coming toward the pool on the grassy pathway. Getting caught meant I would never enjoy the privilege of using the pool again! In a state of near panic, I quickly got out, but thinking I had little time to grab my clothes and put them on, I kicked them over into the honeysuckle and scrambled up the steep path, on the opposite side from which the voices were coming, naked as the day I was born!

Ascending the opposite hill, I knelt down out of sight just in the nick of time. The lady of the house and another elderly woman marched into the clearing. My heart sank, because the thought immediately struck me of how dumb I was *not* to have grabbed my clothes when I had the chance, because I could have been hightailing it out of there! I could see my clothing lying in the weeds from where I was perched, but I doubted the women knew they were there. I surveyed the landscape, surmising whether I could navigate through the brush and retrieve my clothes, but determined it impossible without arousing their attention. Worse than that, even if I could get to them, the way was teeming with wild roses, blackberry thickets, and nettles. Only a garter snake could have made that trip!

I soon discovered that not having my clothes was the least of my predicament. As I hunkered down amidst my woodland wonderland, this giddy pair of cackling females began peeling off their garments like there was a fire sale in aisle seven at Kmart. What they may have imagined to be a back to nature unveiling turned into an outright vexation to my young eyes. This was the last thing on earth I desired as an afternoon's entertainment venue. Their entrance into the pool resembled two ponderous ice blocks, breaking loose from a glacier face, and plunging into an icy fjord. They displaced so much water it sent huge waves boiling out over onto the lawn.

Needless to say, I pondered my situation, but I knew I had gotten myself in a real fix. My only hope was that they wouldn't stay long, and as soon as they left, I could get my things and be on my way to my ballgame. I was kicking myself, knowing time would soon be against me, while trying to think of ways to extricate myself from this mess. I couldn't risk going anywhere in my condition, and I dare not walk down the hill and politely ask, "Excuse me, dear hearts! Would you mind terribly if I fetched my clothing?" I doubt the inquiry would have gotten off the ground before blood-curdling screams filled the forest glade!

I had no choice but to wait them out, yet I could tell by the shadows that the afternoon was fading fast. I kept thinking of how to get home without being seen, while checking back every so often to see whether my options had improved at poolside, but the two nymphs held their ground. I gave the ladies one last fifteen-minute ultimatum, but they were enjoying the amenities of Mother Nature much more than me. I had been roaming the hillside for well over two hours, and my patience was running thin. If I was going to make it to the game on time, I had to leave now. Knowing, finally, what route to take, I left my post and began my risky journey for home.

My first obstacle was an unfarmed field reclaimed by nature, which featured a deer path overrun with dewberry briars, saplings, thistle, and goldenrod. I followed the trail until it ended atop a high embankment, overlooking the main highway leading into town. I stopped to pick an assortment of stickers from my bare feet, which had taken up residence and were anything but pleasant. My nimble fingers quickly plucked them free and relieved the discomfort.

Meanwhile, the cars on the road seemed relentless. It took quite awhile for the oncoming traffic to subside enough for me to gain confidence to attempt the dash across Route 263. It would be no simple feat, as I had to slide down a steep shale slope, race across 40-some feet of hot tar, scale the opposite honeysuckle-covered embankment, and do it in five seconds flat. And this was years before streaking ever became a passion for the lunatic fringe!

Admittedly, I was entertaining second thoughts about my heroic exploits, but the idea of going back through that briar patch, only to find those silly women still frolicking, seemed senseless at best. No, there was nothing appealing about that scenario, and besides, I had already made my decision. I was going through with my plan, no matter what the cost!

In the meantime, my procrastination proved unwise, because my first break in traffic went by the wayside and I was forced to halt my forward progress. When it was safe again, I made my move, and over the top I went, like a possessed Marine. I rumbled down the embankment, ripped across the scalding road, and focused my attention on "Honeysuckle Hill." When I was midway in flight, I realized my decision was flawed. To my dismay, a maroon pickup truck had just pulled out of a driveway a few hundred yards down the road, and it was coming right for me. I hadn't anticipated this, or I would have halted the charge, but like an escaping convict catching his first glimpse of searchlights, I hesitated in the middle of the road in all my glory, evaluating whether to retreat or keep the circus train rolling!

As survival held captive my every thought, I selected "Big Mo"! Stimulated by an adrenalin rush and coupled with a fathomless sense of shame, my bony legs and pounding heart propelled my skinny carcass toward yonder hillside and the promised land that lay beyond. The mad dash landed me in the center of the aforementioned honeysuckle jungle. I commenced a frantic scramble up that slick mound of vegetation and became entangled in the dense tangle of slippery vines. My bare feet and clawing hands proved to be no match for it, but I flailed away at the steep incline, and in a near hyper-hysterical state, frantically inched my way up the greasy slope. My efforts seemed futile, as I felt suspended in time, but I finally reached the threshold and disappeared into the brush, like an arrow into a soft hay bale.

All the while, I kept tabs on the approaching driver, whose identity I did not know, but I was equally certain I didn't give the unknown motorist much to go on either, unless he was able to identify my lily white posterior the way mariners identify whales by their tail markings! Once I gained seclusion in the thick foliage, I took note of the disbelieving stare on said driver's face as he slowed to a crawl, while peering in my direction. I lay on the ground to escape further identification, and assumed he was trying to sort out what he had just witnessed. No doubt, he was optimistically curious how many more of us heathens were sprinting about in "Them Thar' Woods"!

I will never forget the bewildered expression on his face for as long as I live. His mouth was so agape, he looked like a hippo at feeding time! Well, I guess he had seen enough, because he quickly drove on, but to say the least, I was relieved to have left that part of my adventure *behind* me, so to speak.

The rest of my romp was through secluded woodland. There were no more highways to scurry across, so I was anxious to get home and be free of my predicament. I was committed now and I knew I didn't want to dillydally or freak out any more motorists. I also had a sinking feeling the mystery driver might "drop a dime" on me to the sheriff, and I'd best be making tracks.

The section of woods where I trekked soon changed from thick underbrush into a more open stand of trees and dogwood. The forest floor was covered with a soft bed of leaves, which was a welcome relief from the harsh scrub I had been traipsing through. Only problem with the new territory was I couldn't avoid stepping on sticks and twigs. Each one I broke made a crisp snapping sound, which caused concern, because I preferred not to broadcast my whereabouts. To my left was the Parker place and to my right was the Tobin residence. Even though their homes were out of sight, I feared the noise I was making might arouse their dogs. I was quite certain they were confined, but had no desire to get them all stirred up. I no sooner reached that conclusion than the Parker dogs started making a fuss.

There were no other options than to keep going, but I noticed their barking became more intense and seemed to be coming my way. I also knew that they were not small dogs and one had bitten somebody recently. If they were loose, they were nothing I wanted to deal with, especially in my condition. Trying to outrun them was a gamble, so I shinnied up the first dogwood I could climb and straddled a limb about twelve feet off the ground. It was a good thing I took refuge, because those mutts were on me before I knew it, eager to oust me from my perch. They circled and pounced on the trunk of that flimsy tree, doing whatever they could to take a chunk out of my hide.

I probably could have picked a better tree, but there wasn't time to be particular. Although the dogwood wasn't sturdy, at least I wasn't hanging in mid-air with nothing to support me. Precarious and scary as it was, I was high enough that the dogs couldn't get to me; but had I not had sense enough to get off the ground, they would be ripping me to shreds by now, so not all my decisions were empty-headed.

While being safe was reassuring, the commotion the dogs were making was sure to attract attention I didn't need. Then through a small clearing, I could see the stout figure of Mrs. Parker lurking along the edge of her property. She was peering into the woods, looking very desirous to see what her canines were all excited about. This was not a good sign! She began calling her dogs, but they were not at all interested in what she wanted.

If she spots me in this tree, my Lambertville Cardinal days will be over. The next ball I'll see will have a chain attached to it, and the next game I play will be solitaire in a stinkin' jail cell crawling with rats and thugs!

To my good fortune and total disbelief, Mrs. Parker's emphatic commands and hand-clapping carried the day, and her two dogs ambled off in her direction. For the life of me, I couldn't believe those two dogs actually left me hanging there; and better yet, I was alive and well, had escaped detection, and my reputation was intact. But I clung to my perch and didn't come down, until I saw her shut those mangy beasts back in their pens.

With that, I lowered my aching body back to earth and resumed my journey for home. But I realized, at this point, I had run out of time to ever make it to the game, and I knew my plan had totally backfired on me. In fact, not only were things unfolding worse than I had expected, I wasn't sure I'd get home before darkness fell.

In a short while, I was at Rudy Walter's place. His car and truck were gone, which meant he probably wasn't home. Pressed for time, I shot across his yard like a weasel on fire and made short work of that obstacle. I was now two-thirds of the way home, and hoping I could finish the course without any more trials and tribulation. I came upon the path leading from the fort my brother and I had built, which meant I wasn't far from home. I stayed on the path to Hollingsworth's place, which was directly behind our property. For what it was worth, I was relieved to have made it this far in spite of two harrowing, heart-pounding experiences. I had covered nearly three miles and with only a few hundred yards to go, hope gleamed eternal.

The Hollingsworths had two young girls and if memory serves me, they were about five and eight years old. Even though they were next-door neighbors, my brother and I had little to do with them, mainly because the family wasn't all that friendly. More than likely, their mother wasn't overjoyed with the prospects of her little darlings rubbing elbows with a couple of uncouth ruffians like us. Considering the testimony I was displaying, I can't say I blamed her much for her intuition. You don't have to hug a werewolf to know he probably isn't your type!

I crept cautiously down the pathway, crouching low to keep out of sight, and was soon within fifty yards of our back porch. Although progress had been slow, I was gaining confidence with each advancing footstep. Suddenly, I heard giddy screeching and squealing coming from the direction of the Hollingsworth place. It was the Hollingsworth girls. The mother had just turned them loose. Good night! The last thing I needed was another audience or test of character!

Evidently, suppertime was over and Mom had given them permission to go outside and play. What rotten luck! I was so close to our back porch, and now, so far away! I couldn't risk making a mad scramble to our backdoor now, without being seen. Those girls couldn't miss me. This was exactly like the circumstances back at the swimming pool with no place to go! I had been without a stitch of clothing going on three hours. It was getting chilly and the bugs were beginning to pester me. I was in no mood to hide in the shadows any longer, and I was beginning to get desperate. Fortunately, the brush was the thickest where I was cowering, so I stayed put rather than venture into sparser covering, but what bothered me most was this delay and knowing the mother would be watching out the kitchen window.

Meanwhile, the girls were running everywhere, chasing one another, laughing and giggling, like a couple of baboons. As their cavorting went on, I began to wonder how much longer they were going to keep romping around, and how much more I had to remain in my "captive state."

Not only were the mosquitoes getting hungry, every other carnivorous arthropod in the Pennsylvania woods was getting its pound of flesh. I was running out of blood and starting to get hungry and thirsty myself. Comfort was nowhere to be found and my nakedness was gnawing on my conscience.

Growing increasingly weary of the dumb position I found myself in, I came up with an idea. If I could make it to the old doghouse in Hollingsworth's backyard, it was just a short dash to the back of their garage. If I could accomplish that, I would be out of sight and could make it to our side door without being seen. It was decision time once again and the devil was luring me on!

Trying anything seemed better than shivering and being eaten alive, so I decided to end my misery once and for all! Crawling on my hands and knees and out of sight, I scurried behind the abandoned doghouse at the edge of the woods. Peeking around the corner to see where the girls were, I readied myself to make my fourth mad dash of the afternoon, but I never got the chance. Just as I was mulling over whether to abort my idea or go for broke, who should suddenly appear around the corner of the doghouse, but none other than the youngest girl? We both were startled out of our wits! Our eyeballs locked, chills shot up my spine like a Roman candle on a leash, and I'll bet you a meatball sandwich laced with sauce, her little spine was a-tingling too!

I'm guessing she was looking for seclusion in their game of hide and seek, and by the expression on her face, she wasn't anticipating her hiding place to be occupied by a giant white featherless duck! In less time than it took for my jaw to drop, she let out the most blood-curdling scream this side of a haunted house. And let me tell you, my fine non-feathered friends, no human being can scream louder and with more fervency and dedication than a little girl who thinks she's gonna' die! I thought she was going to blow my eardrums out. Still yelling like a bludgeoned banshee, she ran toward the house, just as her protective-minded mother rushed outside to investigate who was getting murdered! "Mommy! Mommy! There's a man out there"! Then, the older sister started to "peel the wallpaper off the wall"!

Not being one inclined to interfere with hysterical women on any level, and fresh out of explanations for why I would be hiding in the woods at twilight, without a stitch of clothing, and with a penchant for terrorizing innocent children, I wasted no time with hauling my sweaty, insect-riddled backside out of there! Parker's dogs seemed like a gift horse compared to the situation I was in now! Hanging from a flimsy tree, with two German shepherds lusting to rip me to shreds seemed like a bargain.

Using the monkey crawl, I tore through the underbrush like an ape making off with a clutch of dried figs. I scampered past my homestead and never ceased escaping until I reached a row of sheds over by the next-door neighbor's property line, where I collapsed in exhaustion up against the musky structure. *I'm done for! I'm doomed*, I thought. *The cops are going to have a field day with me! I'll be in lockdown until they run out of donuts.*

From my vantage point, I could still hear the crying and howling of the Hollingsworth hierarchy, as the father stalked the yard with a club, looking for the slime ball who dared disturb his peace and molest his family. Finding no one to bludgeon, he and his precious harem went back in the house and silence fell upon the land. I stayed put, dreading to move a muscle, and awaiting the arrival of the squad cars to haul me off to jail.

It had been hours since I had ditched my bike and began my seemingly innocent, uneventful march across that cornfield. As I sat there with the evening shadows closing in, I blamed myself for all the trouble I was enduring, but I took heart in the fact that, with darkness, my situation might improve. I would be able to reach our back porch and the sanctity of our living room.

Then, unexpectedly, the Hollingsworth clan marched out of the house, piled into the family car, and drove off, which was a welcome relief to see. It meant I didn't have to stay where I was any longer and I could walk to the house without any worry. As I neared the back porch, who do you suppose should pull up in our driveway? It was Pop in his 1950 Chevy. He got out, carrying a bag of groceries, which meant that he had just returned from the store. Hanging from a wild cherry tree, I called out to him. He heard me, but couldn't make out where I was. I called out again and he beheld my vulnerable state.

I had developed a knack for tree dangling of late, and what better way to demonstrate my prowess than to give an example of my newfound talent? I could sense by Pop's demeanor that he wasn't very impressed with my ability, and from his facial expression, he was having a very decisive conclusion. "That boy has lost his mind!"

I can clarify the situation somewhat, by telling you that he didn't care for my rendition of portraying apes in the wild. I mean, the poor guy had gone through enough hardship in his lifetime, and seeing his #2 son hanging naked in a tree at twilight didn't give him very much encouragement about whether I was going to turn out right and amount to something! I could tell by his pensive demeanor, I would only be wasting my breath trying to explain my motives. "Get me some clothes," was all I could manage to say.

Within minutes, Mom came out the backdoor with a pair of pants and a shirt. My long ordeal was over. I spent several minutes rehashing the chain of events that led to me hanging naked from a tree in Pop's back yard, but I didn't find a whole lot of solace in the telling. So I dropped the subject, knowing I was up a tree in more ways than one, and had learned another valuable lesson from making poor choices.

When school resumed in the fall, I had an assignment for English class in which we were asked to write a three-page essay about something of interest that happened that summer. All I could think to write about was a shorter version of the story I just told you. When I got my paper back, the English teacher wrote the following comments at the top of the first page, "Your punctuation was terrible! Your spelling was atrocious! Your vocabulary needs work! But I never laughed so hard in my life"! A-

Incidentally, after dark, I went back and retrieved my bike, but all I could think about was how humiliating and disappointing the day's experience had been. I knew I had let my coach and team down. We lost the game that night. I really doubt my presence would have made any difference, but the worst part was my credibility with my coach took a nosedive, and things were never the same between us after that. Worse yet, there was no way, in the name of sanity, I dared explain to him my reason for missing that game; and sadly, I never did.

Inner Tube Lady

When my offspring were still in their larvae stage, my wife and I decided to take them to a water theme park over in Rockford, Illinois. Water parks were a new innovation in that day and this one featured a giant wave machine. We all piled in the car with a bulging picnic basket, which was mainly for me and our starving son, who, if we could fend him off, hoped to have enough chow to tide him over until we could make it to the next greasy spoon.

The drive through the Illinois farmland was picturesque. We played car games and sang songs to pass the time. Gretchen and Otto were very creative kids, and in spite of their tender ages, joined us in the frolic with total abandonment. Mary Lou, being a schoolteacher and a *Wheel of Fortune* junkie, demonstrated her sadistic side by bamboozling everyone into participating in one of her favorite traveling car games, "Guess What I Am Thinking?"—which was a formidable challenge under normal circumstances, but she made a complete mystery out of it. This segment of her quirky nature nearly forced me into insanity; because halfway through the first few guesses, her answers didn't always line up with the direction we thought the quiz was taking us.

If she was thinking "horse," for example, and we asked if it was a large animal, she might answer "no," because she was really thinking of a "Shetland pony," but all we were doing was trying to find out how big the creature was. Therefore, our next question might naturally be "Is it smaller than a cat?" She, then, might answer "no," because she would still be thinking of a Shetland pony. At this point, we would be stumped, and it would take quite awhile before we could recover from our bamboozled position. Ah, but that was the joy of the game! It took my mind off boneheaded drivers and flirting with passing milk trucks on hilly, blind curves on the two-lane highway we were nursing!

I located the park fairly easily, arriving shortly after it opened. We hauled in our belongings, rented lockers, and headed for the pools and slides. Lucky me! I stumbled across a twenty-dollar bill fluttering across the walkway leading into the video game area, which helped defer the cost of the expenses and delighted my Germanic heart.

Due to everybody's different aquatic lusts, we went our separate ways, spending time on the water slides, rafts and tubes, sunbathing, and bobbing about in the wave pool. I spent the earliest part of the day battling barrel-rolling bodies in the wave machine and paddling about the wave pool, mindful not to spend too much time in the sun and end up like a boiled lobster.

One of my favorite things to do as a kid when I went to the seashore was to swim in the surf. What I loved to do most was to get out to where the waves were rolling over, and dive in front of the breakers. If I timed it right, the momentum of a wave would take me all the way to the beach. I never tired of doing it, if I was allowed.

Wave machines try to duplicate the action of the ocean waves, but a concrete bottom is no substitute for soft sand. After I got my head slammed into the blue-painted mortar a few times, I gave up on that program; and relegated myself to spending most of my day in the huge Olympic-sized pool, relaxing in luxury, and sipping an occasional beverage at the refreshment stand.

The wave machine operated for half an hour, then shut off for half an hour, to give people a break. Every time it went dormant, the pool population doubled in size, and so did the rafts and inner tubes. The surface was literally teeming with humanity, allowing little room for freestyle swimming; and because of that situation, I spent most of my time swimming beneath the thrashing minions.

I made a game out of the circumstance, by taking a deep breath, closing my eyes, diving to the bottom of the pool, and swimming underwater until I was forced to surface for some air. The game was to see how many times I could surface without colliding with people and their floatation devices. It was a silly pastime, I know, but when you find yourself starved for entertainment, a good imagination can fill the isolation syndrome!

The success rate of my game, at the time of my downfall, doesn't really matter, and I use the term "downfall," because on my next deep dive, I came up inside someone's inner tube. I did not realize that at first, but to my misfortune, the tube had a young damsel inside it, and there was little room left over for unsuspected company. Since the pool surface was teeming with rafts and tubes, and I had managed to emerge topside without incident many times previously; it never occurred to me that in the midst of such tranquility, I would plunge headlong into a murder scene.

To say the least, the buxom damsel didn't appreciate my entrance into her private life, and began swatting me about the head, filling the air with hysterical screeching. At first, I was confounded about what on earth was going on and what I had stumbled into, but it didn't take me long to grab a breath and make a hasty retreat, if for no other reason than to put an end to the pummeling and irrational behavior of my unintended victim.

I swam as far away as my lungs would take me and surfaced on the opposite side, grateful to be alive and free from the melee. I looked around for an angry woman with a piercing stare, but couldn't locate anyone that fit the perception. I considered going back and trying to find her and apologize, but reasoned it wouldn't have helped my cause very much, since I had fled for my life in the first place. I wisely deemed it best to leave things alone, as I doubted my stock was high on her portfolio anyway.

Needless to say, the incident took the luster off of joviality for the rest of the day, but I found other things to pass the afternoon until it was time to head for home. I will confess to being a bit nervous about the incident for quite some time afterwards, half expecting a confrontation of some sort, but was relieved that nothing came of it. I mentioned my experience of "threading the needle" to my wife on the way home, and her response was that I had probably scared the wits out of her. Spot on, dear heart, spot on!

Skunk Heaven

Pop was big on calling a spade a spade. In all my years of dealing with him, he seemed to have an urgency to cut to the chase, especially when his version of common sense hung in the balance. He had no use for highbrow explanations or fussing with particulars. He might beat about the bush when it came to weighing pros and cons, but if you qualified to be a ninny or showed signs of burgeoning idiocy, it didn't take him much time to point out in which category you were gifted. He had no skills in the proper art of narrative descriptions, like you might hear bandied about in British circles of refinery. His verbal explanations usually took the form of brandishing a flamethrower to bag a butterfly. Honesty from the heartstrings of a father can ring the bell of truth at times.

I always had the sense Pop looked at us kids from a guarded parapet, knowing we were chips off "the old block," and fearful of admitting it. When a man grows into maturity and hits mid-stride, the creativity of one's male heirs can trigger moments of frustration, maybe even a touch of envy. The asinine behavior of your kids may bring to remembrance thoughtless exploits you once embraced and fell short of carrying to fruition. As for myself, I have performed some really senseless deeds in my time, but the following leaves no doubt that, in my growing-up years, I could really cross over the line sometimes! Pop's hairy glances from on high were well within reason.

One summer evening, near dusk, when my younger brother and I were crowding puberty, and the katydids were in full symphonic array; we noticed a skunk ambling along the foundation of our garage, and waltz inside. Under normal circumstances, any sensible person would conclude, since it went in there on its own, there isn't any reason why it shouldn't come out on its own; and besides, I can't think of one solitary reason why anyone, with an ounce of horse sense, would want to deliberately stalk a skunk to find out what it's up to—yet, we were suddenly overtaken with the notion we were going to catch that pesky critter and make a pet out of it.

Somewhere along the line, we found out that country folks took these creatures into their folds on occasion. We probably got wind of it from adult conversation that wasn't meant for our ears. The part about skunks having to be "adjusted," in order for this relationship to take place, however, was never properly explained to our youthful, curious minds; and therefore, my brother and I failed to analyze the total concept of our mission. We did grasp the fact that skunks were related to housecats, and that was about all the information we needed to know. Digging in our heels to prove any of the above, one way or another, never showed up on our radar. Quite frankly, in that emotionally-convoluted moment, all we could think about was we had an opportunity to rescue a skunk from the wiles of "Mother Nature," and "Mother Nature" had thrown down the gauntlet.

There was a sad sidebar that went along with all this foolishness, which was our Achilles heel in this situation. That being, we must have been desperate beyond all measure to think we needed a wild animal to cuddle up with at night, like some teddy bear; but we were accustomed to looking for love in all the wrong places, and this occasion was probably no worse off than any other circumstance in which we found ourselves!

Pop's garage was built of cinder block in an "L"-shaped design. His original intention was to have a one-car garage with an adjoining cabinet shop, but he never enclosed it, nor did the woodworking machines ever materialize. Instead, his dream world garage ended up becoming a storage barn at best, with tons of practical junk and rubble he "intended to use one day." In amongst all that organized chaos was where the skunk took refuge.

We knew exactly where it was hiding, because we could see its tail pointing upward, but we didn't have any idea how we were going to capture it, or what we were going to do with it when we did; but we knew we had it cornered. Our first idea was to snatch two clothes props from Mom's washline, thinking the long poles would put plenty of distance between us—to avoid taking a bath in skunk 'urine.' Then we blocked off the doorway with pieces of plywood and an old door to keep our fuzzy friend from scurrying past us. This part of the operation was the only glimpse of genius we had on display that night.

With no cage of any sort to put the skunk in, our brainstorm had taken on an ominous state of affairs, which should have told us something about the outcome of our plot. The back seat of Pop's '36 Chevy came to mind, but we were indecisive as to which one of us was going to pick that critter up and put it in there. We were so busy keeping our new "family pet" trapped beneath Pop's workbench, it never dawned on us how the "old man" would enjoy extracting that thing out of his car, nor his appreciation for having the honor bestowed on him! I'm sure there is nothing more stimulating for an adult, on his way to work first thing in the morning, than to be faced with the prospect of removing a startled, bewildered skunk from your only mode of transport. Even if we got that skittish beast in his backseat, the thought about how much Pop would enjoy his rides to and from work for the next few months never occurred to us, or for that matter, how much the rest of us would cherish riding in the "old bomb," should we carry the day and live long enough to defy his rendition of second-degree murder!

We tried everything we could think of to get that skunk to

give up its hiding place, but I'll tell you what, by the time we were finished poking that nervous polecat with those clothes props, shouting, yelling, banging things around, and scaring the wits out of it, that poor thing's 'pee sack' was so drained, it probably resembled two dried prunes in the Gobi Desert. I don't know how long we kept up our Marlin Perkins's rescue effort, but I'm pretty sure it went on for well over two hours or more. The dedication we had on display that night would have busted the buttons of any school teacher we ever sat under, had we put half as much effort into solving math class problems!

There was nothing within fifteen feet of that skunk that didn't get nailed with skunk cologne, and by that time, I doubt there was any need to get that annoying creature into Pop's car. His upholstery probably reeked like a skunk's den anyway, due to our action-packed escapade, but the odd thing about this whole affair was neither one of us thought we had incurred the wrath of the beast. We figured the stench was just hovering in the air, and we had escaped baptism, but things are not always what they appear to be. You don't learn everything in a math class!

Before long, though, it was getting on to bedtime. We finally looked at one another and realized that we were never going to catch that skunk, but we were content in knowing we gave it our best shot, so we gave up the contest. Mustering all our resolve, we took the barricade down, put the props away, and left the poor woodland misfit to fend for itself. There would be no pet skunks at our house. Disheartened and knowing we had failed, we headed for the sanctity of home, assuming it to be the end of another typical summer night in the life of the Getz kids!

In the event there are those of you who have never had a close association with skunks, or are not acquainted with their anti-social qualities, allow me to educate your mind with a bit of knowledge. Ain't nobody going to hang around a stirred-up varmint like that more than three ticks of the clock, let alone three hours, and not take on the aroma of the second most putrid creature this side of Gag City.

The honest truth is my brother and I had spent so much time in that foul, disgusting environment, we had become accustomed to the aroma. We were clueless our sorry hides smelled exactly like the interior of a polecat. So, when we opened the backdoor and stepped into Dad's serene living quarters, where he was contentedly watching the last few minutes of *Gunsmoke*, he came up out of his easy chair like buckshot from the barrel of an over and under Browning!

"Out! Out! Get out of the house! Both of you!! Get out!!!" he roared. I may not have quoted him exactly word for word, because he was heavily engrossed in determining whether we were ninnies or idiots, and fumbling for proper English, which was a tough expectation when you are gasping for oxygen!

We weren't prepared for his sudden onslaught! I only know he didn't much care for our aromatic fragrance, and you really couldn't blame the guy. We had broken the spell of his inner sanctum. I mean, there he was, totally absorbed in his favorite TV show, doing what guys like to do when the cares of the world crowd in around them. To have his wayward kids fill every crevice of his throne room with a mushroom cloud of skunk fumes was just more than a humble body could take! It just wasn't proper, I tell ya'!

Of course, timing being everything, there we were in the middle of another family ruckus and not ready to meet our Maker. We were just two innocent children returning home after a good old country skunk fight, thinking we were going to wash up, grab a sardine sandwich, hit the goosedown, and get ready for another day; but in all likelihood we could be homeless by sunrise!

Pop's eviction notice was decisive and conclusive, causing us to ponder what he was going to do when he found out his garage and Chevy were no bed of roses either! Degradation and destruction loomed like a dark cloud. We would soon be facing the charging Mongol horde with nothing but a dumb idea and a bad case of hygiene. Once Pop's logic kicked in and he had a chance to evaluate our true asininities and brainlessness, we figured he would run us over like one of Hannibal's elephants! As we stood outside on the flagstone porch, the future wasn't looking very bright. We either had to find that skunk, make friends, and see whether he wouldn't mind having us over for a few days, or start saving our lawn-mowing money for an inexpensive funeral. We were certain we had lost our home.

While pondering all these thoughts, our mom, guardian angel that she was, came out on the porch and told us to take off all our clothes. By this time, Pop had regained some of his composure and we were allowed inside, whereupon they marched us upstairs, while Pop grilled us extensively concerning our fragrant state. Meanwhile, Mom had already started to fill up the bathtub with hot water. When that was done, we were forced to take a soapy bath with Fels-Naptha and vinegar. We went at it for quite a spell, vigorously scrubbing ourselves, until we had taken care of the problem as best we could. Overall, I guess we were fortunate we had a place to hole up for the night. I don't know for sure, but I'm of the opinion to this day, that if it wasn't for Mom's intercession, the outcome might have taken a different twist of fate.

Anyway, the next day, we dug a hole up in the woods and buried all our clothes. We tried to explain our motives to Pop as best we could, but the only responses we could get from him were disjointed mutterings and a mixture of head shakes, which seemed his only reaction to it all. Now that I think about it, there was an element of truth in his fault-finding. Curiously, the one thing about this whole incident is I don't ever recall him mentioning anything about getting the stench out of his car or garage. His silence on the matter has always left me bewildered. Maybe the aromatic scent of "country cat" cleared up his sinuses and headaches, and he opted to keep the secret to himself.

One of these days, when I get to glory, I would love to sit down and have a discussion with the Lord about what He had in mind when He made these smelly creatures. Not that it will matter much what His answers might be, but in all of Scripture, I have never stumbled across polecats mentioned anywhere! Probably, He left them out, figuring they wouldn't need any explanation, which might be God's way of showing us He has a sense of humor. At any rate, it'll be 'gnus' to me, I'm sure!

Tin Can Alley

*I*n the days when our form of government was still our servant and not our master, it was customary for the citizenry to get rid of their own trash. Most folks had a burn barrel or a dumpsite on their property. Burning one's refuse was logical, and it only cost a match or two to dispose of it. If you didn't care for that idea, people shared sites, or you could pay guys like Charlie Rutherford to haul the stuff away. Our tin can dump was out of sight behind Pop's garage, next to the woods, where it wouldn't annoy passersby or us. A few stumps remained from clearing the land, which we used for anvils to smash and flatten the cans. We, in turn, gave them to the scrap man for the war effort. After the war we continued the practice, but every now and again, the can pile would build up. High humidity and Pennsylvania weather teamed up to turn that rusting heap of glittering clutter into an attraction for mosquitoes and a few creatures of the night. Those critters were plentiful, with or without our rustic contribution, but a wise and prudent fellow would lean in the direction of not letting things get out of hand. So, periodically, Pop would put us kids to work smashing up those tin cans with hammers and clubs. My brother and I thought it was great fun, making all that noise crushing and pulverizing things, which was an endeavor we were good at in the first place. Our energies were well-spent, because every tin can we pancaked was one less can Pop needed to deal with, and it diverted our attention away from undermining other projects the "old man" had going on in his life.

My older brother captured a couple of photographs, which we still have in our photo album archives, showing "Slugger" and me, dressed up in our finest can-bashing regalia, joyfully engaged at our task. They are some of the most "classic" snapshots we have of our earliest days in Solebury.

One of the funniest and most phenomenal memories I have of this account was we would sometimes drink sips of stagnant water out of those old cans. Some of that gory liquid would have a sweet taste to it, but *NOT* every time! I guess the experience had just enough appeal to it, we kept checking to see if we could find another batch to our liking. I don't know whether we drank those mystic elixirs of our own volition, or somebody put the "I dare you" idea into our heads in order to try and "liquidate" us. If you understand anything about sibling rivalry, anything is possible. I know I could see myself urging my younger brothers to "Go ahead, it won't hurt you"!

In any event, it was a wonder of wonders we never came down with some deadly disorder and croaked before the next sunrise. Pondering it now, the idea makes my skin crawl just thinking about it. I, alone, probably downed enough mosquito larvae to rescue Bucks County from an outbreak of yellow fever five times over. I'm no medical expert, but those "inoculations," most likely, are the reason my brother and I developed such good immune systems! We probably contracted rare mutations of typhoid, botulism, malaria, and plague, but never showed any signs of assuming room temperature. I suspect those early experimentations greatly altered our brain waves, stifled our common sense, and left us vulnerable to fits of delusions, but they preserved us long enough until we were rescued from ourselves by matrimonial ties!

Scratch Where It Itches

It's a raw deal to be in the right place at the wrong time. I am persuaded some calamities come straight from the Pit, because I'm sure the Creator doesn't waylay us just for the fun of it; but then again, lightning strikes skunks as well as stray kittens. Whatever the case, I know for sure life gets ugly in a hurry when you're blindsided by Providence. It would be nice if we lived in a perfect world, but we wouldn't have any yarns to spin.

This story takes place when I was right in the middle of an ugly divorce from my first trial run with matrimony. I arrived home from my drill press job, eager to take on the world. All I remember about that hideous night was that I had been in a big rush to go nowhere. I felt no need to pamper myself with perfection, so I flung my work clothes in the general direction of the clothes hamper, the top of which had broken off a few weeks before and was dangling in mid-air by one hinge. Using typical masculine logic, I figured if my cruddy garments failed to make it inside, I intended to straighten up things when washday rolled around, because the "maid" wasn't fussy!

I rummaged around in my bureau drawers for some clean underwear, but like most disorganized bachelors, all I could find was a tee shirt with seven holes in it, and a catcher's mitt. It occurred to me I had taken all my dirty clothes to a Laundromat the night before. Like a wild man, I searched through my pile of clean rags, stuffed in a big cardboard box, which served as a laundry basket. I will thank all you heckling critics to hold back your derisive laughter, as desperate men do desperate things, rather than caring what they're planning to wear for a meaningless night out on the town. Concerning my laundry basket, let's just say I had an attraction for cardboard boxes, and economics occupied the high ground in my life at the time! Plus, it was important for me to make an impression on the old gals folding clothes down at the launderette. You don't want to give them snarly old women any ideas that you may be "well off," or they'll start sizing you up! Anyway, I came up with a set of "undies" good enough for the occasion, so what more can you ask?

In that day and age, it was customary to look nice whenever a fellow went out, even if it was just to pop into a grocery store for two cans of baked beans and a flounder filet. Donning a shirt and slacks, I had just finished cinching up my shoelaces when I noticed that my skin began to itch here and there. At first, I didn't pay much attention to it, only thinking that it seemed odd; but by the time I splashed on some cologne and was ready to storm out the door, the itching had become very intense around my waist, shoulders, and especially near my groin. Within seconds my entire body was "alive," as if a thousand tiny bugs were biting and stinging me everywhere. I tried to ignore the intense itching, but the more I scratched, the more irritating the situation became.

I had no idea what was going on, but I needed to do something to relieve the problem, because the itching was driving me crazy. For a moment, I thought I would gut it out, but common sense overruled my inclination by the time I reached the front door. Whatever the problem was, I needed to put an end to it quickly!

In desperation, I raced back to the bathroom like a thoroughbred and shed my clothes, because the itching had become unbearable. I couldn't believe how fast the affliction was advancing. For a few moments, I was uncertain what to do, and was becoming more concerned by the minute. I started to think maybe I had contracted some rare disease, because on top of all the itching, I began to experience cold chills from head to toe.

I remembered that I had recently bought some oil of wintergreen, which I had intended to rub on my muscles after softball games, but hadn't had a chance to use it. I don't know why I didn't just buy a regular body rub. Maybe I figured if a little wintergreen was good, full strength stuff was better. Anyway, not knowing what oil of wintergreen really was, I worked in a generous amount of oil to the areas giving me the most trouble. At first, the elixir brought some soothing relief, and I was glad to have put an end to the madcap discomfort, but the serenity didn't last very long! The mint substance began to grow warm very quickly, and the warm feeling soon intensified to a burning sensation, which escalated into a raging fire, and before I could say "Holy Smoke!" my skin was aglow! The areas where I had rubbed in the wintergreen oil became a literal inferno. In fact, my skin felt as if I had been branded with a Triple-D B-bar-B branding iron!

Let me be expressly clear when I say, there are very sensitive areas of my body that I never want to have set on fire, let alone doused with molten coals. Biting deerflies and shin kicks I can deal with, but firebrands do nothing for my low-key Sagittarian disposition!

Like a dog whose tail had been slammed in a door, I shed my clothes and sprinted for the shower stall. It was the only self-preservation I could even think of to do. I turned on the controls, fumbled for a cake of soap, and began frantically lathering myself, until the cool cascading water brought some relief to my harried carcass. Wherever I had applied the wintergreen oil, my skin was as red as a beet. I stood under the shower twenty minutes or more, continually lathering myself, until I experienced any level of comfort. What a relief! It was as if I had escaped a burning building or something.

When I dried off, I drenched myself in baby oil and talcum powder, and donned a new pair of "Skivvies." After dressing again, I headed off for my destination, quite leery of any new signs of itching, but peace had been restored.

The first thing I did when I got home was dump the oil of wintergreen down the drain, because I couldn't come up with one solitary reason why I wanted to be branded like a longhorn, or set myself on fire again! To my knowledge, I have never used wintergreen rub, chewed wintergreen gum, or gargled with wintergreen mouthwash since. When I retold my experience, several people mentioned that someone must have thrown fiberglass curtains in the washer I used, before I did my laundry load, and never gave a second thought about the next customer!

I tossed all of my underwear in the trash, because of not knowing which ones were safe to wear! "Heavens to Murgatroyd," I didn't want to travel down that road again! "Timing is everything," as they say, and this was one time I got that message!

Calm Down, Florence, It's Green, Ain't It?

Growing up in a small town as my brother and I did, it was second nature to learn the "lay of the land." Once we outgrew the familiar surroundings of our yard and bordering woodlands, the urge to explore the "regions beyond" became an all-consuming mission. We used every opportunity to venture farther and farther from our apron strings. In time, our curiosity discovered where the best cherry trees grew, what kind they were, and whether we could get to them. We kept an eye out for when they ripened and scaled whatever heights we had to, risking life and limb, in order to acquire those succulent, worm-riddled "gut flushers"! If buckshot was on the menu, we reasoned it wasn't in our best interest to get our rear ends air-conditioned, just to spit pits in our midst.

We also figured out where the sweetest wild strawberries grew, who raised the domesticated "honkers," and whether they could be had. However, the "highbrow stuff" was more of a challenge for our culinary cravings, and brought a different set of obstacles into our method of operation. Most of our challenges were not for the faint of heart! True liberty, my friend, always has a price tag connected with it! The domestic berries were usually well-guarded and just as sought after by the owners as us marauding Getz kids. The difference between our two interests being, we weren't particularly keen on getting ourselves electrocuted, ripped to shreds by dogs, leaping off shed roofs, or outdistancing property owners wielding pitchforks, clubs, or Remingtons; but if the thing to be gotten featured a glimmer of hope and the lure loomed relentless in our minds, I'll bet you a dozen Hires' bottle caps, we would give it our best shot to rescue whatever it was from *being wasted.*

It was on this pride-filled premise, my fifth-grade teacher happened to ask if anyone would volunteer to bring in a Christmas tree for the class to decorate. Few situations ever presented themselves whereby I could become a hero in the eyes of my prepubescent peers. Come to think of it, there wasn't a whole lot of humanity beating down my door to bestow the honor on me either. Seizing the moment, my hand shot up like a milk snake latching onto a Holstein's udder.

"Can you get a tree for us, Dennis?" asked Mr. Stevens, eyeing me with a piercing glare of skepticism and expectancy. I nodded in the affirmative.

"Well, this is great! I guess that takes care of our dilemma. Thank you, Dennis," he acknowledged.

Why is it that some people never know when to keep their mouth shut? I don't know either, but ten seconds after I had sold myself down the river, I was kicking my rear for being so dumb. First of all, I didn't have any trees. Secondly, "snagging" Christmas trees was risky business, but due to the fact I had just made myself out to be "The Masked Marvel," I realized I had just doubled my yearly quota and upped the ante of getting my neck stretched! One thing was certain, I didn't dare break my word and squash my classmate's hopes and dreams. In the space of twenty seconds, I had gone from a model citizen to a candidate for reform school; not to mention my good-heartedness didn't exactly capture the Christmas spirit in a nutshell. Let's see! How does Christmas gift-giving go? Oh, yeah! Go cut down somebody else's spruce tree that doesn't belong to you, and give it to a bunch of ungrateful renegades for a present!

No wonder our childhood Christmases were so dismally grim most of the time! God was more merciful than I imagined! It was a miracle lightning didn't shoot down through the rafters on Christmas Eve and ignite our humble dwelling into a burning inferno!

Even though I was only 11 when this story got its legs, my brother and I had been snagging Christmas trees for our beleaguered old man ever since we were old enough to wield a hatchet and drag a saw through the snow. The truth was, we knew Pop had pretty much soured on the idea of partaking in the gaiety of Yuletide celebrations. Thanksgivings took a lot out of him before we ever got there, and yes, there were exceptions when he would interrupt the pattern; but usually whenever Christmas rolled around, a combination of morbid economics, foreboding woe, and "bad vibes" influenced him to denounce all frivolity connected with that hallowed holiday. He generally embraced a more sinister outlook regarding the event. During those delicate and sensitive mood swings, I didn't have the finesse to pry into his conclusions, but part of the problem arose from the fact my brother and I worked tirelessly to destroy the old man's serenity on a regular basis, leaving little chance to smooth him over when it came time to barrel down the homestretch into the joyful festival of lights!

Another way of stating this comedic situation might be, if you happen to be a stallion, and horseflies are gnawing on your flanks all the time, you aren't very partial to horseflies! The very notion that Pop would spend his hard-earned cash on spruce trees in the dead of winter, let alone put trinkets under them for two bothersome kids who generated a steady stream of patrol cars up his driveway all summer, coupled with a parade of irate neighbors demanding compensation for pranks and deranged behavior, was incomprehensible. We stood a better chance of whipping Pop into a good mindset for Christmas by tossing a box of shotgun shells into the downstairs coal furnace! As you can see, gift-giving was a dilemma in our household!

But regardless of our deep-rooted Christmas traditions, every single year we were under Pop's roof and still able to draw breath, my bro and I were undaunted in risking life and limb fetching them sap-riddled conifers. In our hopeful imaginations, if there was any chance of bribing Santa into springing for our cause, his inspiration might blossom if he had a green-needled, tinsel-laden fir tree sticking up in the middle of his living room floor!

About a mile from our house was a dense, overgrown thicket, entangled in honeysuckle, which I always thought had once been a tree farm and pastureland. It guarded the western edge of town and was dotted with cedar, black locust, briars, and the evergreens we sought. It was a creepy, foreboding place, with one concentrated area where dozens of enticing Christmas trees grew. We knew of no other acreage where they could be found in such numbers. The majority of them were more than twenty feet tall and very grotesque, but some featured nice tops, perfect for any quaint Yule setting. But because there was no practical way to climb up and cut the tops out, they were worthless to us. However, sprinkled in among these wild giants, several smaller trees could be found, hemmed in on every side and difficult to see. That never deterred us from sniffing them out, though. Like any good bloodhound, we found our quarry in spite of the odds against it.

Our plan was to visit this "gold mine" in late October, select what we thought would suit us, and make a note of it. Then a week before Santa Claus blew into town, we would sneak off at dusk with one of Pop's newly-precision-sharpened Disston handsaws and capture our prize.

Naturally, whenever one of these escapades was concluded, we would return Pop's crosscut saw back to his carpenter's toolbox, thinking he wouldn't notice anything was disturbed. As a token of our appreciation for the use of his A-1 cutlery, we would manage to coat the handle and saw blade with a generous supply of sticky pine sap. There was little doubt that this benevolent gesture proved to be the mechanism for propelling our "old man" into another killing mood the next time he needed to use it. These "special moments" in his life always gave him one more reason to fill our stockings with mud, and stymied any shred of Yuletide joviality he may have been clinging to. Allow me to elaborate on this theme, because the mental picture I'm getting is too precious to waste by keeping silent.

Our dad was a master carpenter by trade. His expertise was staircase-building and a sequence of complicated trim work his employer usually called upon him to perform. This required a great deal of precise figuring and the use of a variety of hand tools. Pop spent hours filing and sharpening his chisels and handsaws, bending each tine and honing each blade "just so." Whenever he needed to make a precise cut on a piece of oak or cherry, his saws would slice through these hardwoods like butter, straight and true. Can you imagine his frame of mind, upon reaching for one of his prize "weapons," under time commitments and tension, only to discover the handle covered with sticky sap and multiple saw teeth gummed up with pine tar?

"Bloody" Mary had nothing on him when it came to issuing death wishes during those exasperating sequels! I just know his endearing offspring crossed his mind during those momentous occasions. Gallows, guillotines, and visuals of diabolical lynching and bloodletting must have flooded his consciousness, as we shared with him our version of free enterprise; while proving, once again, we had violated one of his cardinal directives, "You kids keep your hands off my tools! You hear me?"

I envision Pop's seething rage, having to spend the next half hour cleaning up his beloved saw with turpentine, only to find out when he was done, that his venturesome, marauding sons not only had cut down a Christmas tree he didn't want, they had sawed halfway through a granite rock while hacking down a neighbor's tree in the darkness, rendering his faithful Disston hand tool totally useless! Ah! The blessings of childbirth!

Meanwhile, back at the ranch, I broke the news to my younger brother that this year we needed to extricate two trees when we made our raid, because I had made a deal to get one for my classmates. As this objective was no deterrent to him, we assembled the tools of our trade, waited for nightfall, and went calling on the unsuspecting citizenry.

As the darkening shadows of an early December twilight chased the brighter shades of daylight, we began our fearless trek through cornfield stubble and hedgerows toward our foreboding destination. We reached the edge of the overgrown woods and made our way to where we thought our selected tree was located. Our instincts were correct, and we wasted no time felling the object of our affection. Soon, darkness claimed the evening shadows and only a few wisps of pink clouds clung to the far horizon. With daylight fading more quickly than we had expected, we decided to end the search for another tree and dragged our reward through the underbrush, until we reached the main road leading home.

Each time a car came up the road, we realized two kids carrying a Christmas tree in the darkness, a few days before Christmas, and dangling a handsaw, might give a deputy sheriff cause for concern, so we sought the security of the gutter, taking our Christmas tree with us. After three or four ditch dives, we decided the next time a car came by, we would stand the tree up alongside the road and hide behind it to cut down on the "sweat factor." Within moments, another car came up over the hill, and we stood the tree up and took refuge behind it. It worked! The driver couldn't see us! In our minds we reasoned we were clever fellows, but I doubt we fooled anyone. Why would a tree be growing two feet from the edge of a road and have five trunks?

In a few more days, Christmas vacation began to draw down on me, and I hadn't yet come up with the tree I had promised. Several classmates were getting impatient and began hurling derisive remarks in my direction. When Mr. Stevens expressed his concern too, I knew I had to get the production lines rolling. I promised, when I left school on Friday, that I would have a tree first thing Monday morning, as school let out the following Thursday.

During early dawn the next day, my brother and I found ourselves back in the grove looking for the second tree. We weren't concerned about heading into the woods, but coming out with our trophy would draw the most attention. In truth, we didn't think anybody would really care about what we were doing, but to be safe, we decided to make our selection, cut it down, and come back for it at twilight. A light covering of fresh snow covered the ground; just enough to make tracks and cause us some misgivings, but we foraged around until we found one suited to my liking. We hadn't been in the grove very long when we thought we heard voices. We froze, listening intently, wondering if our minds might be playing tricks on us, but our hunch was right. What seemed like a few dozen yards away came a deep, husky voice, "Look! Tracks! They're in here, alright!"

I looked at my brother and he looked at me. We both had the same aghast expression. It's the look a woman might get the moment she spots a wolf spider crawling up her arm, while enjoying the amenities of an outhouse! The reference to "tracks" might have meant rabbits, for all we knew, but we weren't sticking around to discover the difference!

Our lower extremities were already underway, and our rear ends and fidgety feet soon joined in. The thunderous stick-smashing exit out of that woods wasn't exactly as dainty as two young fawns might have done it, but we cleared the cornfield and made the main road in fine style. We may have appeared a trifle suspicious, barreling towards home, with Pop's saw flapping in the breeze and guilty looks on our faces, but the native populace was accustomed to the Getz kids hightailing it somewhere in a big ole' hurry. Should anyone have inquired about our hectic flight, no doubt we would have come up with some brilliant excuse like "We were cutting ice blocks down at the river when a pack of wolves jumped us!"

When we arrived back home, the realization that I would not be bringing a Christmas tree to school that year began to dawn on me. There would be no hero's welcome as I had envisioned it either, only ridicule and humiliation, which is what I dreaded most. There was no way I was going to venture back into that "hornet's nest," and try my luck of snagging a tree now. It just wasn't worth the trouble, plus, I had a sense of honor rolling around in my misguided heart of hearts. It was one thing to be a sneak, quite another to be a premeditated crook. I had standards, you know!

I found myself gazing out the upstairs window, feeling downcast and trapped by my circumstance, wondering where on earth I was going to get a Christmas tree. I began to pace the floor, trying to come up with a solution, but couldn't think of anything within reason. I remember pausing and looking westward, out of the window, toward Uncle Emil's sawmill. How was I going to face Mr. Stevens and those cannibalistic classmates of mine? In the depths of my quandary, I continued to stare out the window at the snow-covered field and the dozens of cedars growing helter-skelter across the landscape. Then it hit me! *Wild cedars!!!*

"Hey, Florence! They're green, aren't they?" I heard myself thinking. Florence was one of the ringleaders who came up with the tree idea in the first place. *"You want something to hang popcorn on? Bammo! There it is, baby!"* What a revelation!

Within minutes, I was out in the cruel snow-covered world, dragging back to the house one of the most gorgeous specimens of coniferous junipers mankind had ever laid eyes on. It was a ten-foot beauty! Minutes later, I had that hatchery for "praying mantis" standing against the back porch, ready for delivery. It was a master stroke of sheer genius, or so I thought.

Proudly and heroically, I hauled that spiked leviathan off the back porch, down the road, across the schoolyard, and into the classroom, first thing Monday morning. I stuck it up against the blackboard before the main contingency of protagonists arrived. There it was! My pilfered contribution to all Christendom!

Mr. Stevens seemed delighted, as were the few students that were already there, but I was as nervous as a convict awaiting execution on death row. Soon, the school bus arrived with the rest of my classmates. They began to file into the room and the long anticipated fantasy of becoming "1951 Hero of the Year" was at hand. Sure enough, even before half of those ungrateful goons ever put their books down, derisive, cutting commentary filled the air and things grew ugly in a hurry. Spiteful remarks like "meathead" and "idiot" flooded my ears. "That ain't no Christmas tree!" also filled the halls of academia. It seemed to me there wasn't one solitary soul who ventured forth a kind word on my behalf. All I could think of was all the trouble I had gone to for those kids, but I suppose I deserved everything their accusations implied. My premise was dead wrong from the start, and my executioners knew a real Christmas tree when they saw one! Guilty as charged!

Fortunately, Mr. Stevens came to my rescue and thanked me for my effort, which was just before the kids found a rope to lynch me. His intervention saved the day, because he had the wisdom to size up the situation and recognize the uncomfortable position in which I found myself. He ordered everyone to take their seats, settle down, and be grateful they had a tree.

When the morning recess came, the "decorating committee" begrudgingly adorned my skinny aberration with all the handmade ornaments, et cetera, until that green, hairy stalk didn't look half bad, especially when all six limbs had tinsel hanging from them.

When all was said and done, that Christmas turned out to be the worst one I ever had in my entire life! Not only did the classmate who drew my name for the gift exchange elect not to get me anything, the ill-gotten tree my brother and I brought home didn't impress Santa one iota either. When we came downstairs Christmas morning, the only objects under the boughs of that tree were fallen needles, cobwebs, and a sleeping yellow cat. The coup de grace, which I believe was the Maker's way of telling us we needed to "shape up," was the absence of a gift from Aunt Ruth and Uncle Harold, who never failed to "spring for us" at Christmas. Consequently, there was absolutely nothing to open; not even a piece of candy!

For an eleven-year-old kid and all the anticipation leading up to the event, I was crushed; but do not feel sad for me, because I received a gift that year no amount of money could ever buy! The guilt that I carried, the humiliation I earned, and the dejection I felt caused me to do a lot of soul-searching. The Lord took me to the woodshed and I realized my despair was of my own making. If memory serves me right, that was the last time my brother and I ever took a spruce tree out of that woods. Lesson learned!

The other highlight to come out of that experience was it put an end to the intrigue surrounding "The Case of the Sticky Saw Handles."

About the Author

Dennis R. Getz served his country in the U.S. Air Force. He also worked for the U.S. Postal Service for 25 years. He was actively involved in his church community and a longtime member of the Harmony Hawks. Dennis and Mary Lou Sheldon were married in 1973. He had three children, Paula, Gretchen, and Otto. Dennis was a gifted writer, who wrote many short stories and poetry that he enjoyed sharing with family and friends. He was a dedicated fan of open wheel dirt track racing and the Cleveland Indians. Dennis also loved his dachshund, Dottie. This book of his whimsical recollections is dedicated to his memory, with love, from his family.

Made in the USA
Lexington, KY
26 November 2014